LEGACY
OF
RESILIENCE

PATRICIA A. PAPE

authorHOUSE®

AuthorHouse™
1663 Liberty Drive
Bloomington, IN 47403
www.authorhouse.com
Phone: 1-800-839-8640

First published by AuthorHouse 1/4/2011

ISBN: 978-1-4567-1041-5 (sc)
ISBN: 978-1-4567-1040-8 (dj)
ISBN: 978-1-4567-1038-5 (e)

Library of Congress Control Number: 2010918439

Printed in the United States of America

Any people depicted in stock imagery provided by Thinkstock are models, and such images are being used for illustrative purposes only. Certain stock imagery © Thinkstock.

This book is printed on acid-free paper.

Because of the dynamic nature of the Internet, any Web addresses or links contained in this book may have changed since publication and may no longer be valid. The views expressed in this work are solely those of the author and do not necessarily reflect the views of the publisher, and the publisher hereby disclaims any responsibility for them.

To my grandchildren

DISCLAIMER

This is my story. I have told it as I remember it, to the best of my ability. The opinions or thoughts are my own. I know that everyone does not see the world through my eyes, but I've done my best to write the truth as I see it. I can't decide what is true for others. My intent is to share only my own truth. Therefore, I take responsibility for my thoughts, feelings, opinions, and conclusions. What I hope to do is gain a greater understanding of my ancestors and gain an awareness of their strengths. I also hope to give a sense of pride to my grandchildren as they realize their own *Legacy of Resilience* that comes down through our family.

CONTENTS

PREFACE

THE DARK DECADE

How can dark and light coexist so closely together?

When I got married in 1962, I was blissful and sure that the future held everything I could ever want in my life. In reality, there were some wonderful moments in the next decade, but also some of the most tragic times. My two children were born in 1964 and 1966, and what blessings they were! But I also spent most of my time during those ten years either drinking or in blackouts from drinking. There was emotional and verbal abuse, which escalated, as did the drinking. But the abuse and drinking were separate issues, neither of which was the cause of the other. And I had to deal with each one separately.

However, when I made the decision on March 22, 1972, to walk away from the years of abuse—and, with the help of friends, poured out the last bottle of cheap sauterne—I was frightened and ashamed. I knew I had to leave my marriage, and I did so, but with a great deal of fear and trepidation. I had never lived on my own. How would I make it? I didn't have a job, and I had no source of income. Yet

I knew deep inside me that this was what I had to do. I needed to leave the darkness behind and walk toward the light, even though I had no idea what that future might bring. I didn't know if God, my family, my friends, or even I myself could forgive me for all the awful things that had happened during that decade, but I was committed to finding out.

And so I began my own inner pilgrimage, which continues today, thirty-eight years later. I believe I have learned to be more accepting of the fact that darkness and light can coexist closely, in the same person, the same lifetime, and the same universe. I thank God each day for leading me on this adventurous journey toward the light.

Lovelines are the threads that carry the strengths of my family through the generations. The threads of Aunt Sadie's doiles, which I will discuss later, are examples of these lovelines.

Resilience is another one of the threads that runs through my family's stories. I define resilience as bouncing back from something and moving on. That something usually involves a wounding, suffering, or loss. Resilience involves healing, learning, and transforming. One purpose of suffering is to learn from it. Mistakes are not negative if we learn from them. That thread of optimism and hope runs throughout our family stories as we continue to learn from our pasts, especially regarding compassion for others.

I believe that my ancestors did the best they could—loving their children and grandchildren and passing along some healthy values and personality traits. But the alcoholism and violence in my lifetime made it difficult to see the good fruit on the family tree. It sometimes takes an outsider to point this out. That, for me, was Christina Baldwin at the workshop on Whidbey Island last summer. As I lingered with the one-hundred-year-old pictures of Bonnie Guy and my other ancestors, I began to have a sense of their love and caring, although each of them showed this in different ways.

I searched for the story line of strengths that come through my family. This took time because the negative memories were much stronger than the positive ones. But this sense of being loved began to emerge, and with that I am now able to focus on the positives and the resilience in my family. This is my whole purpose for writing this memoir and passing it on to my children and grandchildren with love. We are all given choices. We all need to take charge of our lives, work out our own faith statements, and move forward to fulfill our purposes for being placed on this earth.

I have learned that *family* goes beyond bloodlines or shared last names. I talk both personally and professionally about a "family of choice." Those people who love and support me are my current "family." I picked a surrogate mother and a surrogate father, and I have written about both of them. My faith community and my spiritual life continually challenge me to grow.

Actually, I learned to pick "family members" when I was very young. My father was an only child, and while my mother had two stepsisters, they lived in Ohio and California. So we had "adopted" aunts, uncles, and cousins with whom we spent the holidays. Once again, I learned that family is not a name but is about love and caring.

One of the unexpected benefits of writing this memoir is gaining a new perspective on my family. One of my favorite pictures is of my father, mother, and me when I was perhaps two years old. I was leaning with my cheek on my father's cheek, and I can feel the love that I now realize he had for me before he became sick with his own disease. I am hoping that sharing this story with family members will result in healing for many. Who knows? All I know is that I feel I *must* write this story. I am grateful to God for guiding me so far.

This book is dedicated to those who have ever thought they could not overcome the past problems in their families. We all have the resiliency to overcome much that challenges us from our pasts. Let me show you some of the strengths, love, and resilience that came through my family.

ACKNOWLEDGMENTS

Dorothy and George Bryson helped me begin this journey over a decade ago. They are experts in genealogy, and Dorothy has helped me acquire numerous documents. They have driven me to cemeteries in both Illinois and Indianapolis, Indiana, to locate family graves. I am grateful for all their help.

Sue Oldham Baughman and Nancy Oldham LeCompte, for all of the pictures and information they provided.

Barbara Peck, research assistant for the Aurora Historical Society, for all of the documents and information she provided.

Mary Ann Pirone, for her help in searching old newspapers and other documents at the Aurora Public Library.

Lauren Master has been my computer angel, helping me so many hours to perfect the manuscript. She has worked even when her back was killing her and the pages went on and on. She has also listened to me read many of my anecdotes and made wonderful suggestions.

My other computer angel has been Fred Amundsen. He has been so faithful in his availability when I e-mail him and write, "Help! I don't know what I've done!"

My writing friend Penny Foiles has made numerous suggestions over the years and has been so supportive when I felt like throwing in the towel.

My writing friend Tom Germuska took the first chapter with him on the airplane on his trip to Texas in order to give me feedback.

Christina Baldwin and all the writers from the Whidbey Writer's Group have continued to challenge and support me in my first writing attempts.

Denis Ledoux and his *Turning Memories into Memoirs* class taught me a great deal about how to write a memoir.

And finally, I am grateful for my nine grandchildren, for whom this book is written.

INTRODUCTION

JOURNEY INTO THE FOREST

Tears are running down my face as I finish reading a letter to my grandpa Hanks and also my Fairy Tale Story about my childhood, both of which I wrote early this morning, before our class started. It is June 21, 2009, and I am sitting cross-legged on the floor in the circle of twelve writers, under the leadership of Christina Baldwin, at the class The Self As the Source of the Story. I am discovering that what I thought was just a seminar to learn how to be a writer will initiate a journey of self-discovery and culminate in the writing and publishing of this book. I am wearing my large light blue hooded sweatshirt that says THE MARSH HOUSE OF WHIDBEY ISLAND. It has kept me feeling safe and secure this entire week as I attend my first writers' conference and read some pieces about my past, taking risks with these women I hardly know. Their comments are so accepting and nonjudgmental that I feel the healing that is occurring. Little do I know at this moment that during the next nine months, I will go back into my past heritage many times, but from a new perspective.

Dear Grandpa Hanks,

You died April 22, 1940, and I was born August 2, 1940, not quite four months later. I have cried many tears this week because I never met you and you weren't part of my life. Salty little tears are dropping out of my eyes and running down my cheeks and onto my paper right now, for lack of knowing you.

I look at the picture of you and Grandma Hanks with Aunt Lois when she was two. You have on a white dress shirt and gray slacks. Your hands are folded in your lap, and you are looking slightly down instead of directly at the camera. All my pictures are black and white, so I don't even know what color your hair and eyes are. They appear to be brown.

Your skin looks perfect, soft, and unblemished in any way. You are so handsome; do you know how lovely you are? Your lips are always closed. Sometimes you look like you might smile, but you don't. Do you flirt? Do you like to tease? Are you playful?

Your eyes look so kind, deep, and gentle. Were you a gentle spirit? You were only seventeen in the picture with your Aurora Zouave hat and tassel on. Were you proud of being a Zouave, with your blue jacket, red fez, and light blue vest? The *New York Journal* said your drill team looked like a "huge red-legged centipede," marching 220 steps per minute with your Springfield rifles.

My mother, Helen Louise Hanks, was a loving, soft, and gentle spirit. Did she get that from you? What did I get from you? Was it your love of adventure? I know you traveled around the world, performing for royalty and excited crowds, with the Barnum & Bailey Circus. Your winter engagement in Vienna, Austria, reminds me of being there also, in 2003, to present on Spirituality and Alcoholism for the International Council on Alcohol and Addictions Conference.

You are the reason I am doing this project. When my cousin Sue Baughman sent me several of the old family pictures that she thought I might like to have, I found your picture with "Pratt Photo, Batavia, Ills" imprinted on it. I got so excited. Batavia is twenty minutes from my house. Then I discovered that you were born in Copley Hospital in Aurora, Illinois, as was I, just sixty-six years later. Did you lead the way for me? Would you have loved me, your little granddaughter, as I love mine?

When I read about your being in the Aurora Zouave World Championship Drill Team, I thought how proud you must have been to be the United States national champions and to march for President Grover Cleveland and then for the queen of England. Did anyone in your family attend your performances? I wish I could have been there to shout and cheer for you. I would have been so proud of you.

Thank you for all that you valued (kindness, gentleness, passion) and passed on to me.

I love you,

Patsy (your loving granddaughter)

Feedback from Christina Baldwin on Grandpa Hanks Letter*

It's always been a theory of mine that for a person to survive psychically, somebody has to be there. There has to be at least one life in a child's life. And it can be a teacher or a neighbor—somebody has to turn around and say, "I see you." And, in a way, it's Grandpa Hanks. Even though he was not physically present, it's like he died and became your guardian angel over your childhood. You know, because you have these profound feelings for him and longing for him. And I see you paying attention to that, and noticing, and looking for how to wrap language around this relationship that has been so significant in your life without having a way to speak it certainly in reality.

The other thing is to really go into looking at those moments of love, in the midst of all the alcoholism and the incredible falling apart of human life, that you have this photo of you leaning your cheek against your father. It's amazing.

So there's still a thread in there of real attachment that hasn't been completely destroyed by the addiction. And you had the sophistication to do that because of who you are—not only the life story you carry, but that you listen to all the time. So hold that up for yourself.

Even the question "Do you know how lovely you are?" could be one that you ask yourself. Often the things we notice are things as we are, not as another is.

And your alcoholism was the gift of love from your dark side. There was nothing you could have ever done to deserve it.

The threads of alcoholism, real attachment, and resilience shine through all of your story.

*From the class The Self As the Source of the Story, June 2009, Whidbey Island, conducted by Christina Baldwin. Her website is www.peerspirit.com.

ANCESTORS OF PATRICIA ANN GROVER

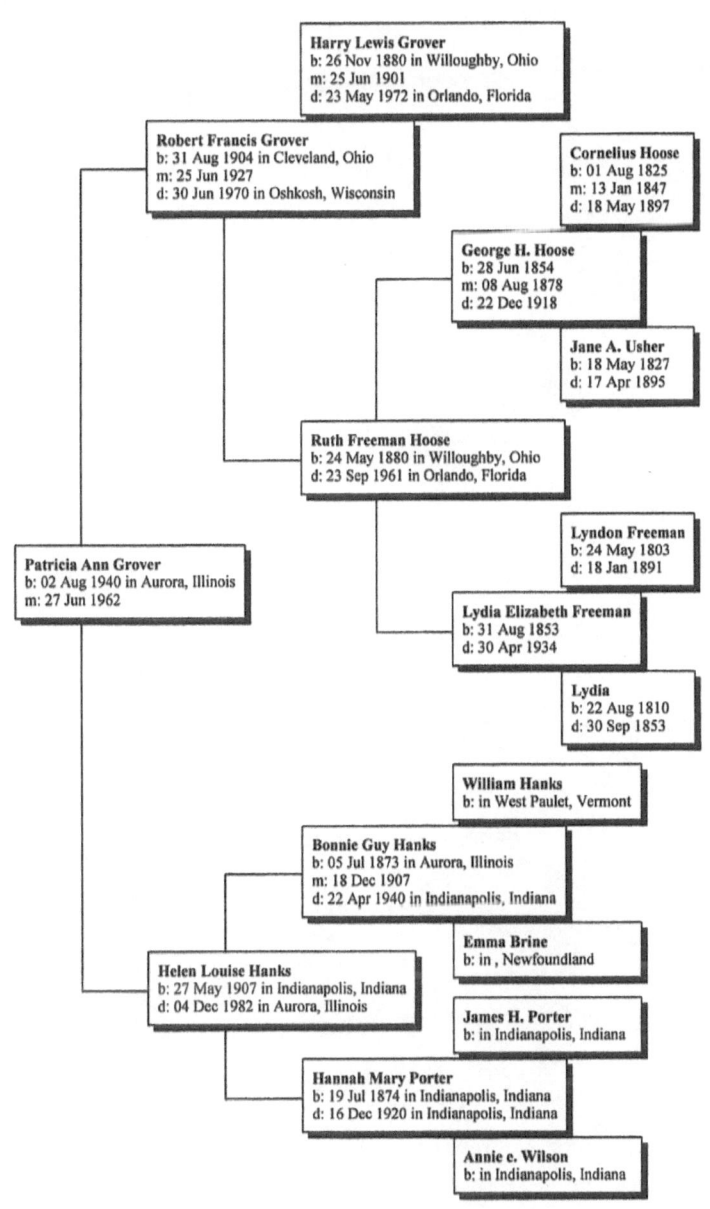

Harry Lewis Grover
b: 26 Nov 1880 in Willoughby, Ohio
m: 25 Jun 1901
d: 23 May 1972 in Orlando, Florida

Robert Francis Grover
b: 31 Aug 1904 in Cleveland, Ohio
m: 25 Jun 1927
d: 30 Jun 1970 in Oshkosh, Wisconsin

Cornelius Hoose
b: 01 Aug 1825
m: 13 Jan 1847
d: 18 May 1897

George H. Hoose
b: 28 Jun 1854
m: 08 Aug 1878
d: 22 Dec 1918

Jane A. Usher
b: 18 May 1827
d: 17 Apr 1895

Ruth Freeman Hoose
b: 24 May 1880 in Willoughby, Ohio
d: 23 Sep 1961 in Orlando, Florida

Lyndon Freeman
b: 24 May 1803
d: 18 Jan 1891

Lydia Elizabeth Freeman
b: 31 Aug 1853
d: 30 Apr 1934

Patricia Ann Grover
b: 02 Aug 1940 in Aurora, Illinois
m: 27 Jun 1962

Lydia
b: 22 Aug 1810
d: 30 Sep 1853

William Hanks
b: in West Paulet, Vermont

Bonnie Guy Hanks
b: 05 Jul 1873 in Aurora, Illinois
m: 18 Dec 1907
d: 22 Apr 1940 in Indianapolis, Indiana

Emma Brine
b: in , Newfoundland

Helen Louise Hanks
b: 27 May 1907 in Indianapolis, Indiana
d: 04 Dec 1982 in Aurora, Illinois

James H. Porter
b: in Indianapolis, Indiana

Hannah Mary Porter
b: 19 Jul 1874 in Indianapolis, Indiana
d: 16 Dec 1920 in Indianapolis, Indiana

Annie e. Wilson
b: in Indianapolis, Indiana

THE HANKS FAMILY

In 1993, my cousin Sue Oldham Baughman, who is about five years older than I am, sent me several original pictures of my maternal (Hanks) side of the family. Suddenly, a whole new journey developed. I found myself yearning to get to know Bonnie Guy Hanks, my grandfather. This is some of what I found.

I have traced the maternal side of my family tree, the Hanks family, back to the first member of that family to arrive in America.

In 1699, Uriah Hanks, the first of my ancestors that I have any information about, traveled across the ocean from Birmingham, England. His family started the first silk mill in the United States in Mansfield, Connecticut, on Chestnut Hill, later known as Hanks Hill, where he built their spacious "Mansion House." Says one source, "Great men were produced under such hardships." Uriah is described as a man of great piety and ingenuity. Rodney, the youngest of his nine children, was a mechanical genius with great perseverance. An 1872 article in the *Hartford Courant* was entitled "A Family of Inventors." Benjamin, his oldest son, started the first bell and cannon foundry in America. His daughter remembers such famous men as Aaron Burr and Ethan Allen very well, as they visited her father often.

I have a letter from my uncle Marrian Oldham. Entitled "About the Hanks Family," it reads as follows:

> Geraldine and I went to Ford's Greenfield Village the second week in July 1940, where we visited the first silk mill ever built in America. We were surprised to read the following inscription: "First silk mill in America." Erected at Hanks Hill Connecticut, just outside Mansfield in Tolland County by Rodney and Horatio Hanks. It was driven by water power. Benjamin Hanks, their great-grandfather, came to America in 1699, and as early as 1768, the Hanks family was in the silk business. They built other mills, the last one being erected in 1882.

It was signed M. S. Oldham.

I think it must have taken perseverance, resilience and hope for my pioneer ancestors to survive and thrive.

Early in the eighteenth century, Benjamin's son William Hanks moved to Pawlett, Vermont. His son Urunah had seventeen children, the oldest being William C. Hanks, my great-grandfather. William moved to Aurora, Illinois, where he is listed in the 1870–71 Aurora Directory as a carpenter (R. R. shops) and in 1905–06 as a carpenter for the CB&Q Railroad. I just learned that the CB&Q (Chicago, Burlington and Quincy) started in Aurora. In 1866, he married Emma Elizabeth Brine from Newfoundland.

I feel proud of my heritage and some of the traits I believe I inherited from these people: inventiveness, ingenuity, and the spirit of entrepreneurial adventure. I always wondered how these people all ended up in Aurora, only blocks from where I was raised two generations later (on Downer Place), born in the same hospital (Copley), and working in the same geographic location (CB&Q and Love Brothers). It must have been a job with the railroad that drew my great-grandfather to Aurora.

William C. and Emma E. Hanks had four children: Bessie, Jerome, Roy, and Bonnie Guy, my grandfather, born July 5, 1873.

The Hanks families each had ten or more children. In his 1940 family genealogy, Jerome writes that the "record is that the Hanks families were very prolific."

Bonnie Guy was a member of the U.S. Champion Zouaves Drill Team when they took first place in Burlington Park, Illinois, in 1890, and national first place in Indianapolis, Indiana, in 1891.

Bonnie Guy married Vida Delight Fink in Aurora on January 1, 1896. They had two girls, Lois in 1902 and Geraldine in 1904. It had to have been difficult when Vida died January 14, 1907. But in true Hanks fashion, he carried on and moved with the two little girls to Indianapolis, Indiana. He married Hanna Mary Porter, "a wonderful person," according to what was written on the back of the picture of Lois and Geraldine standing in front of the house in Indianapolis.

I wonder if Bonnie Guy moved into the house of James Mullen (Hannah Mary Porter's father-in-law) at 1943 Broadway. I'm also curious to know if Harry and Ruth Grover (my paternal grandparents) lived nearby in their "Broadway apartment in Indianapolis," as quoted in our family home movies. Is that how my parents met? Did they go to school together? So many unanswered questions.

My mother told me almost nothing about her childhood. She did say once that the family were Christian Scientists, and therefore no one would call a doctor for her mother. Is that a true story? In 1929, Bonnie Guy was listed in the Indianapolis directory as a certified Christian Scientist practitioner with an office at 41 Washington, Indianapolis, Indiana. I think it must have been hard to bury a mother/wife on December 16, 1920, the week before Christmas. How sad it must have been to disrupt the anticipation with a funeral. And what a tragedy if lack of medical care was part of the reason.

How did he start over with three wives, two of them dying? Was he lonely? After marrying Hannah Mary Porter, my mother was born. He was a Christian Scientist practitioner, according to the 1929 census records and Yellow Pages. How did he do that and still make enough to support his wife and three daughters? What did he do after Hannah Mary died in 1920, when my mother was only eleven? In 1930, the phone directory lists him as a public accountant, living with Belle, a practical nurse and his third wife. Perhaps he abandoned his Christian Science practice after losing two wives.

On October 29, 1931, my uncle Roy E. Hanks's obituary was written in the Aurora *Daily Beacon-News*. Called one of the city's star bowlers, and charter member of the famed Aurora Zouaves, he was a credit manager and cashier of the Aurora Corset Company. He was also a charter member of Aurora Lodge No. 705, B. P. O. of Elks. Roy was educated at the Aurora public schools, as was I, and lived on LeGrande Boulevard, a few doors from where one of my best friends lived during my lifetime. Why didn't I ever hear about these uncles, aunts, and cousins? Surely my parents knew they lived there.

We visited Grandpa and Grandma Hanks' graves in Crown Hill Cemetery in Indianapolis. Hannah Mary is buried in the Porter plot, next to her first husband, Amasa J. Mullen, MD. Grandpa Hanks's grave was all alone under a tree, with no headstone. I felt sad. And once again I wished so much that I had been able to get to know him. The Lovelines coming through Grandpa Hanks are strong threads of perseverance and resilience, and I want to always be aware of them. I am like him in so many ways.

Hanks Silk Mill in Mansfield

Hanks Hill Silk Mill
Far left: John S. and Ozro Hanks, owners

HANKS SILK MILLS

I have traced the maternal side of my family tree to the Hanks family, early American producers of silk.

Uriah's oldest brother William sent to England for some mulberry trees, planted the first trees in Connecticut, raised the first silkworms, and made the first handmade silk in the colonies. Uriah himself persevered until he made silk culture (sericulture) a successful business in Connecticut. Sericulture is the breeding and management of silkworms. Uriah's younger brother Benjamin invented a silk spinner, which was patented.

The Hanks Silk Mill in Mansfield was built by Rodney and Horace Hanks in 1810. It was only twelve by twelve feet in size. Rodney was Uriah's tenth and youngest child. In 1810, Mansfield was an agrarian community. Silk production was done in the home, unraveling the cocoons by hand. By 1830, Mansfield led the county in silk production, and silk manufacturing had moved from the home to the factory. This was typical as the United States moved from an agricultural to a manufacturing country. The Industrial Revolution had arrived.

In 1848, the wages of men averaged $1.14 a day; of the women, $0.63 a day. The average was $0.72. Another interesting fact was that the public library of the town developed from the books that were read to the girls in the skein room while they worked. There was no machinery, so the girls could easily hear the reader as they unreeled silk from the cocoons for hours on end.[1]

The great significance of the Hanks Silk Mill was its utilization of water power. This was the first step toward mechanization in the American Silk industry. Recognizing this significance, Henry Ford purchased the building in 1930. It was reconstructed in his Greenfield Village Museum in Dearborn, Michigan, where it can be seen today. In fact, this is the very mill, with its inscription, that my Aunt Geraldine and Uncle Marrian Oldham saw and wrote about in July 1940, the month before I was born.

William's granddaughter, Harriet Paloubet,[2] remembers seeing her grandfather in his black coffin at his funeral. She was five years old. She remembers that he had no teeth and his nose nearly touched his chin. Her grandmother Hanks lived with them after his death, until she fell on her face on the red-hot coals in the fireplace and was burned to death. Her father, Joseph, caught the fever of the Western emigration. He sold all he had and started in midwinter, with ten children, one only three, for the far-off land of Ohio, the land "flowing with milk and honey."

Harriet says, "My father was a self-made man, his father holding that a child must live and work till he was of age, without schooling or a trade or a calling for his future life, in order to pay his parents for his bringing up. My father, longing and thirsting for knowledge, would, in passing the schoolhouse, linger outside, and finding a strip of paper with a copy of writing on it, take it home and try to imitate it. He later bought a book called *The Young Man's Best Companion,* by diligent study of which he became a respectable scholar."

The Hanks Brothers Silk Mill advertising card shows the four successive silk mills built on Hanks Hill. The first water-powered silk mill in this country was built in 1810 by Rodney and Horatio Hanks. In 1821, Rodney Hanks built another mill, located across the road from the first one, and was joined by his son, George R. Hanks. A new and larger mill was constructed on this site in 1854. George Phil and John S. Hanks took over in 1858. It was named P.G. & J. S. Hanks Company. After fire destroyed the mill in 1882, a fourth mill was built on this site and operated until 1928.

Silk Mill and employees, Hanks Hill, November 13, 1907. At the far left are the mill owners, John S. and Ozro Hanks. Note the hanks of silk hanging to dry on the left.

1. Manchester, H. H., *The Story of Silk and Cheney Silk,* Cheney Brothers, South Manchester, Connecticut, 1916.

2. http://familytreemaker.genealogy.com/users/c/a/r/Kenneth-Gene-Carpenter/BOOK-0001/00 …

Mansfield Historical Society:
http://www.mansfieldct-history.org/silk_production.shtml
http://www.mansfieldct-history.org/hanks_mill.jpg
http://www.mansfieldct-history.org/silk_mills_tour.shtml

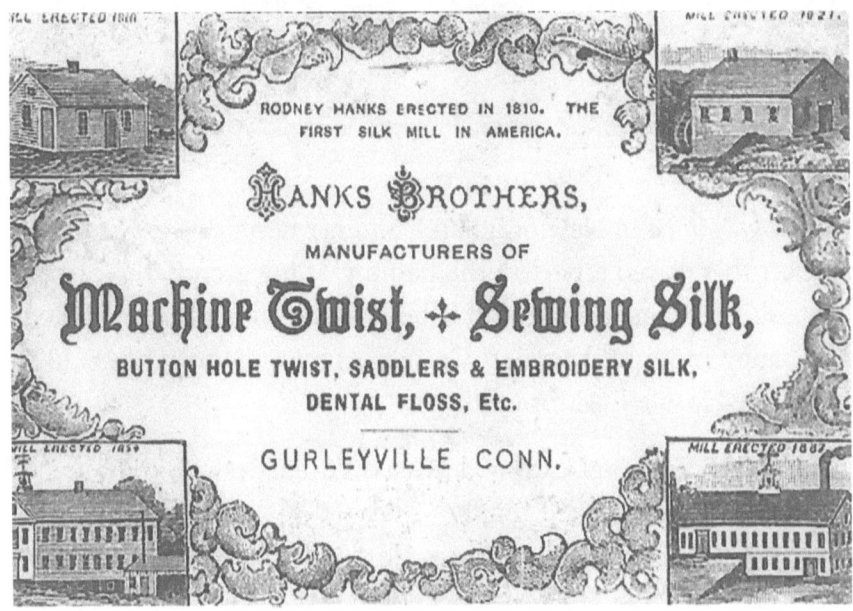

SCOTTISH LAD

Emma was born in Newfoundland, and her heritage was Scottish. I suspect this played a part in the naming of my grandfather. In the Scottish tradition, a bonny lad is best, beautiful, and perfect. He is also happy, fun, and charming. Grandpa Hanks was born July 5, 1873, in Copley Hospital, Aurora, Illinois.

William and Emma already had three children, Bessie Bird, Roy, and Jerome. William worked for the Chicago, Burlington and Quincy Railroad in Aurora. He and Emma Brine were married in 1866.

THE AURORA ZOUAVES*

by Vernon Derry

The Aurora Zouaves were organized in August 1887, with G. A. Hurd as Captain. Their first interstate drill was at Kansas City, Missouri, in June 1890. They took third prize, due to poor equipment and uniforms. They managed to secure good uniforms and Springfield rifles and challenged all Zouaves companies in the United States for the championship, which they won that year. Captain Hurd led his drill team to many honors, including drilling before President Grover Cleveland in 1892.

Under Albert Tarble, in May 1896, they won the title of "World Champions." They were immediately signed with the Buffalo Bill Wild West Show in Madison Square Garden, New York City, in April 1897. The reception in Madison Square Garden before 15,000 was epic-making. The drill team was termed the greatest company ever and many historic appearances followed.

The Aurora Zouaves uniform consisted of a blue jacket, red fez and pants, gold sash, white leggings and a light blue vest. According to the *New York Journal,* the Aurora Zouaves were "a huge red-legged centipede, whose marvelous precision have astounded the military men in town."

In 1900 the Aurora Zouaves signed with the Barnum and Bailey Circus for the winter in Vienna, Austria.

*Reprinted with permission from *Thrift Corner Yarns,* Volume 21, March 1963. Published by Aurora Savings & Loan Association.

Aurora Zouave jacket was blue, fez and and pants were red, gold sash, white leggings, light blue vest.

Hurd's Island after winning First Prize

In a compact squat group, at the rate of 220 steps per minute, the Zouaves moved in an ever-widening circle while becoming erect.

Climax of Aurora Zouave's exhibition was scaling a twelve-foot wall in eleven to eighteen seconds with their fourteen-pound Springfield rifles.

Bonnie Guy Hanks

Roy E. Hanks

BONNIE GUY HANKS MARRIES
VIDA DELIGHT FINK

Bonnie Guy was eighteen and a member of the U.S. Champion Zouaves Drill Team.

He was married to Vida Delight Fink on January 1, 1896, by E. W. Louusbury, a minister. Vida was born in Davis, Illinois, to John F. Fink and Mary C. Nagle. Witnesses were Jerome Hanks and William E. C. Pratt. Given their names, they must have been very happy. They had two girls, Lois Delight in 1902 and Jessie Geraldine in 1904, my aunts.

I look at their pictures and admire their beauty. Grandpa Hanks had such engaging eyes and perfectly combed hair. Vida was lovely in her high-necked dress; she had flowers on her shoulders and in her hair. What an attractive pair they made.

I suspect Bonnie Guy dropped out of the Zouaves after he got married.

What a shock it must have been when Vida died of peritonitis January 14, 1907. She was buried in Spring Lake Cemetery in Aurora, Illinois. Her gravestone is in error, stating that she lived 1873–1906.

Grandpa Hanks moved with his two little girls to Indianapolis, Indiana.

BONNIE GUY HANKS MARRIES
HANNAH MARY PORTER

These two pictures are special to me. They were two of the first pictures my cousin Sue sent to me. They were both taken in 1908, which makes them over one hundred years old. This is written verbatim on the back of the left-hand picture: "Lois and Geraldine Hanks, 1908, Indianapolis, Indiana, as we arrived to live with our Dad and new step-mother Mary Porter Hanks—a wonderful person."

The right-hand picture is of Bonnie Guy Hanks and his second wife, Hannah M. Porter Hanks, with my aunt Lois sitting in the middle. It was summer 1908, and my mother, Helen Louise Hanks, was born May 27, 1909. My grandpa looks happy and proper in his white shirt, bow tie, and gray pants. Grandma Hanks is just barely looking up, a smile playing on her lips. Aunt Lois looks happy in her fancy dress. She has a bow on her head, and her hands are folded in her lap.

Grandpa Hanks was an accountant living in Indianapolis, and Grandma Hanks lived with her parents at 1943 Broadway, Indianapolis. My uncle Adolph Seidensticher was the witness of the marriage, which took place on December 18, 1907. They too were a good-looking couple.

How sad it must have been when, at forty-six years of age, she died on December 16, 1920, from chronic parenchymatous nephritis. My mother was only nine. How did Grandpa Hanks cope with being a widow again, this time with three young girls? Grandma Hanks was buried in Crown Hill Cemetery in the plot of her father, James H. Porter. She was buried on December 18, the thirteenth anniversary of her wedding. And so close to the Christmas holidays.

ROY E. HANKS

Every time I think I have learned all I can about the Hanks family, something new is added to the mix. Yesterday Dorothy Bryson and I went to the Aurora Historical Society, and they had two boxes of pictures, invitations, booklets, and articles about the Zouaves. And then we went to the Aurora Museum downtown, where they had an actual Zouave uniform. I was so excited to go that I could hardly sleep the night before!

Roy E. Hanks was born August 25, 1871, two years before Bonnie Guy, and he died October 28, 1931, at age sixty, at his home at 241 LeGrande Boulevard. We went to see the old brick house where he lived and died, just nine years before I was born. According to his obituary, he was one of the first to join the Aurora Zouaves, and he toured with Buffalo Bill's circus around the world. I have a picture of Roy with the Buffalo Bill Wild West Show at Madison Square

Garden, April 1897. According to the article, bedlam broke loose from the fifteen thousand present, and it was some time before they could begin their drill.

The Zouaves were not allowed to gamble, use intoxicating liquors, or debate on political or religious issues. They formed a brotherhood that lasted for the duration of their existence. Bonnie Guy and Roy would have been in their late teens when they marched with this group.

Roy was also a charter member of Aurora Lodge No. 705, B. P. O. of Elks. I can still remember my father taking us to the Elks Club on Friday nights for dinner. I never knew that my Uncle Roy had been part of this group. As with many of the Hanks, Roy seemed to enjoy branching out and trying new things, a trait I enjoy myself.

We also found the probate information for Harriet L. Hanks, signed by Kenneth R. Hanks on August 21, 1933. There is a two-page list of chattel property, including an icebox for $5.00, a double bed for $5.00 and twin beds for $7.50, a blue rocker for $0.60 and an Essex sedan automobile, 1929 model, for $50.00.

Roy and Harriet had two children—Helen Hanks Reising, born in 1901, and Kenneth R., born in 1905—and one grandson, James Reising, all of Aurora.

Bonnie Guy and Roy look very much alike in their side-by-side pictures. Both are handsome, both serious, not smiling. I wonder what was going on in their minds. I am assuming that Bonnie Guy may have stopped traveling with the Zouaves when he married Vida Delight Fink in 1896.

GRANDPA HANKS—TWO FACTS

I think it is unusual to have only two facts from my mother about her father:

1) "Your grandpa Hanks had perfect teeth! He never had a cavity in his entire life," she told me, probably during one of those times that I was complaining about how hard it was to clean my teeth when I had braces. My father used to tell me that they always took good care of my teeth and feet. I am guessing this gives me a clue to their value system.

2) "Grandpa Hanks was the secretary of the YMCA, yet he never taught his own daughter how to swim," my mother said. I can remember her in her blue satin bathing suit with the little skirt, jumping in the tiny waves in the Atlantic Ocean, at Daytona Beach, on one of our trips to Florida to visit Grandpa and Grandma Grover. But if the water was deep,

she wouldn't go near it, almost like the old nursery
rhyme "but don't go near the water!"

Both of these are curious little facts, especially since they are about all she told me about her father. I wonder why she didn't tell me more. And the part about his perfect teeth is especially interesting to me because in his pictures he never smiles, never shows those perfect teeth.

AUNT SADIE'S MEMORIES

When I was a little girl about ten years of age, I loved to spend time in the attic, going through old pictures and items from the past. My parents loved to tell the story about the time they had gone to their potluck supper group and our babysitter, Mrs. Miller, called them, frantic, and asked them to please come home right away because "Patsy is in the attic, and it is over one hundred degrees up there, and I'm afraid she is going to have heatstroke!" And so my father came home and dragged me down from the heated room where I had already spent a couple of hours.

One of the things from the attic that I found fascinating was a large box of old items from my great-aunt Sadie. The black leather cover of my aunt Sadie's small three-ring diary is tattered and falling apart. Most of the pages are coming out of the three rings, even though she put round reinforcements around the holes. Every page is typed. The newspaper articles about family members are attached to the pages with the same little white reinforcements. In her own handwriting, she wrote: "This part is for Pat if she cares for it. If no one wants it, destroy it. Sadie F. Hoose."

12939

597

WARRANTY DEED

This Indenture Witnesseth, *That*

Lillie E. Hoose, unmarried,

of Marion *County, in the State of* Indiana
Convey and Warrant to Sadie F. Hoose and Ruth F. Grover, their
heirs and assigns forever, of

of Marion *County, in the State of* Indiana , *for and in consideration*
of Love and affection **Dollars,**
the receipt whereof is hereby acknowledged, the following described **Real Estate** *in*
County in the State of Indiana, to-wit:

An undivided one-half interest each of the grantor's one-half
interest in lot 228 (Two hundred twenty eight) in Northcroft second
section, being a re-subdivision of Lot one (1) to twenty five (25)
inclusive in Hartman's Broadway addition to the city of Indianapolis,
the plat of Northcroft second section appearing of record in the
office of the Recorder of Marion County, Indiana, in plat book 14,
Page 66 thereof.

Subject to the unpaid balance of a certain mortgage for Six-
thousand dollars ($6,000.) drawn in favor of the Fletcher Savings
& Trust Company, dated December 4th, 1922 and recorded in mortgage
record 840 page 406.

Subject to the unpaid balance of a second mortgage for twenty-
five hundred dollars ($2500) drawn in favor of the Standard Investment
and Securities Company, dated December 7th, 1922, and recorded in
Mortgage record 839, page 360.

Subject to the 1924 taxes due and payable in the year of 1925.

The said Sadie F. Hoose, unmarried, shown as grantee above, was,
at the time prior to the making of this instrument the owner of an
undivided one-half of the above described real estate, being a
tenant in common with the grantor named herein.

Property Deed

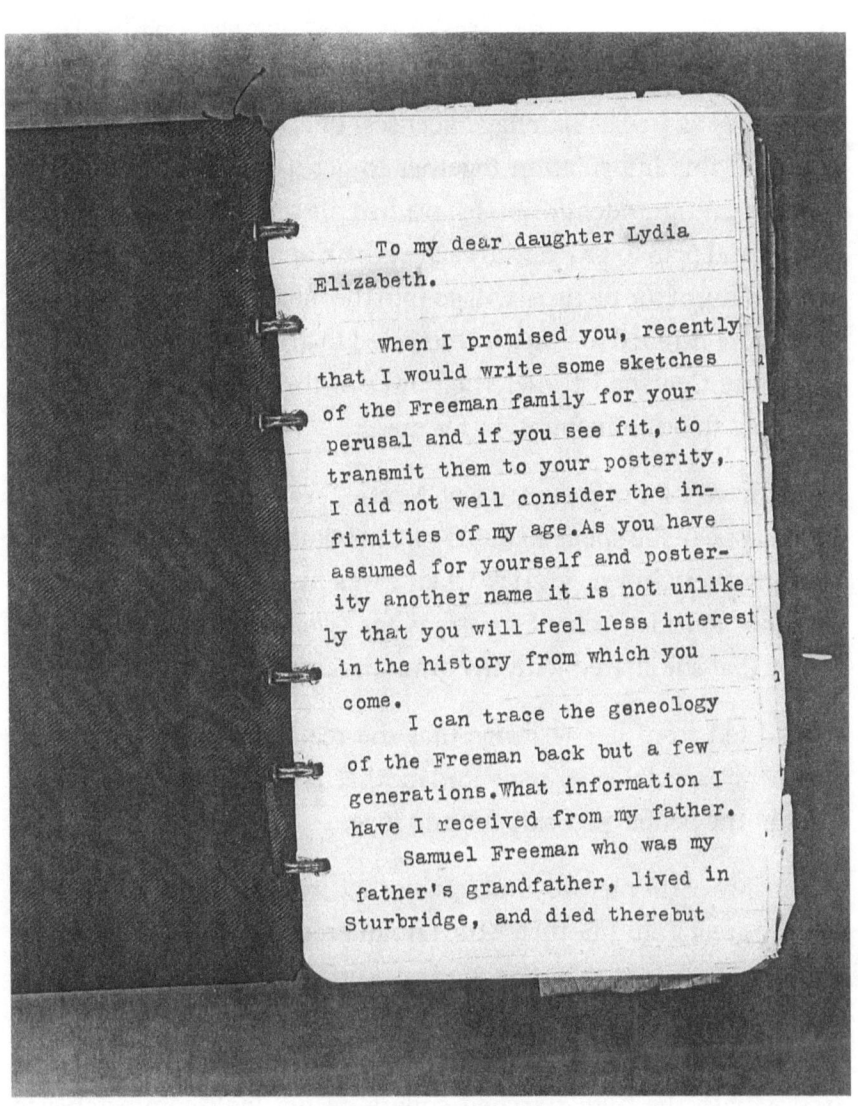

To my dear daughter Lydia
Elizabeth.

When I promised you, recently
that I would write some sketches
of the Freeman family for your
perusal and if you see fit, to
transmit them to your posterity,
I did not well consider the in-
firmities of my age.As you have
assumed for yourself and posterity another name it is not unlike
ly that you will feel less interest
in the history from which you
come.
I can trace the geneology
of the Freeman back but a few
generations.What information I
have I received from my father.
Samuel Freeman who was my
father's grandfather, lived in
Sturbridge, and died therebut

Aunt Sadie's Diary

And so I inherited all her diaries, her handmade doilies, her important papers, and her pictures of the Hooses, the Freemans, and the Grovers.

About ten years ago, my friend Dorothy Bryson, a genealogist, began to help me research my family heritage. We sent for birth and death certificates as well as marriage licenses. I began to think about how to put all this information together to get it into the hands of my children and grandchildren. I have had all the doilies restored and framed and plan to give one to each of them at my seventieth birthday party. Many of the pictures will go into the memoir I am writing. And so I have continued to remain connected to great-aunt Sadie through the doilies that she left me. The power in the threads of the doilies continues to be an inspiration for me.

I don't have a lot of memories of Auntie. From the home movies, it would appear she spent a couple of Christmas holidays with us. My grandmother Grover got sick when I was five, and we used to go to Orlando, Florida, every Christmas for two weeks and stay in her duplex that she shared with my grandparents.

I could tell from her writings that she really cared for her family members, especially her sister and mother. She taught me that family is about the people you care for and love.

I am in awe of the pictures and frames that are over one hundred years old. My great grandmother, Mrs. Lillian Freeman Hoose (Lillie), was born on August 31, 1853. She died on April 30, 1934, six years before I was born, and was buried with her family in Mentor, Ohio. The full and formal hairdos, the high and fancy hats, and the stiff-looking dresses with the high-starched collars do not look comfortable to me. She married George H. Hoose, who was born June 28, 1854, and died December 22, 1918 (many of my family members died at Christmastime). They were married August 8, 1878.

Two of the sweet things that I highly prize are warranty deeds to two properties, carefully described in legal terms, in Marion County, Indiana. They "convey and warrant these properties to Sadie F. Hoose and Ruth F. Grover, their heirs and assigns forever, for and in consideration of love and affection Dollars, by Lillie E. Hoose, Unmarried." Isn't that something?

"Auntie," which is what we called Sadie, describes the last year with her mother, the houses they bought and sold, and her medical treatment at the end:

> Mother and I moved to 1362 E. 115th St. from Mentor on June 1, 1919. We lived there until May 1920. Then, having sold our place at about double what we had paid (prices were high), we bought a two-family house at 1628 Elsinore St. East Cleveland.

> Ruth's folks lived upstairs and we down until March 1921, when they moved to Indianapolis, Ind. E. B. Hoover and family occupied the upstairs until after we sold in July 1, 1923. We sold our house at N. Lockwood to R. G. Campbell and the Elsinore Place to J. Bowen. Did well with both.

> Moved to Indianapolis, July 1, 1923. Harry (my grandfather) had bought a bungalow at 624 E. 49 St. before we came. We like it very much.

> Bought a double house at 4910 and 12 Broadway for $12,000.

> Aunt Nell came to Indianapolis the last of Sept. and moved into Ruth and Harry's house the first of Nov.

MOTHER'S LAST YEAR

Mother and I were together from October 1933 until she passed away. We had a splendid time together. She missed not being able to get out but became quite reconciled.

Robert and Helen were here nearly every Sunday for the evening meal, and either Monday or Tuesday dinner.

Mother had some cold after I did and a little asthma but the doctor pulled her out of those in quick time. He prescribed port wine, and it helped so much.

But later she did not feel well, and another bottle of wine did not do what the first had done. She had been taking digitalis, and consequently her stomach was bothering her. Her feet also swelled. Doctor was in Saturday afternoon and prescribed the clear liquid that had always done so much for her. We were so encouraged. She slept well and seemed better in the morning (she had had quite severe attacks of breathing).

Sunday she got up late. While I was pressing some summer dresses for her, she went to the bathroom. She came back to the davenport, sat down, and had a terrible time breathing. When I reached her, she had had a stroke (10:30 AM). She was conscious and wanted the doctor. I could not get Warfel at once (Lukenbill would not come). Dr. Warfel got here finally about 11:30 and gave her a shot that relieved her. After a second one, we got her into the big chair. (Mrs. Green was good). Robert and Helen came about 3:00 PM. Mother asked if he had sent for the folks and seemed contented after that with Robert and Helen. Mrs. Pearce came in to see if anything was wrong and was the last neighbor she knew. Mr. Yockey and Gene helped her back into her chair, and Doctor and Robert got her into bed about 5:00. We made her as comfortable as possible. She pressed my hand and knew me at 11:30. After that she became unconscious and never rallied.

Robert and Helen sat up until 11:30 and I until 4:00 AM. I was so glad I could.

We got a nurse, Miss Ogden, the next morning, and Mom left us at 3:00 PM Monday, April 30, 1934.

I am struck with the detail, the love, and the concern. I am also impressed that the doctor made house calls. I love it that he prescribed a bottle of wine, and that it did so much good. I can remember many a time that my mother gave me "warm whiskey water" for my cramps. Those old medical remedies may have done as much good as the more expensive medicines of the day. But the above diary entry of Aunt Sadie is typical of her coverage of people's illnesses, deaths, and burials.

Sadie saved all the obituaries and newspaper accounts for Grandma and Grandpa, and then someone saved hers. I learned a lot from these obituaries, although it seems like a strange way to learn about your family. Ruth Freeman Hoose Grover, my grandmother, was born May 24, 1880, in Willoughby Ohio. My brother Jim was also born on that date. A lot of us were born or married on each other's important dates. Grandma died September 23, 1961, in Orlando, Florida, and was buried in Willoughby Cemetery. She belonged to the First Presbyterian Church (I thought they were Seventh-day Adventists) and also the Mitzpah Chapter No. 190 Order of Eastern Star, a Masonic organization, in Orlando. I also belonged to a Masonic organization, Job's Daughters, in Aurora.

Harry Lewis Grover, my grandfather, was born November 26, 1880, in Willoughby, Ohio, and died May 23, 1972, at age ninety-one. He was buried in Willoughby, Ohio. He was the secretary-treasurer of English Woolen Company in Willoughby for fifty-one years and moved to Orlando in 1945 when he retired. He married Grandma in Waite Hill, Ohio, June 25, 1901 (that is also my parents' wedding anniversary). He was a member of the Orlando Lodge 69, F & AM and the First Presbyterian Church. He lists survivors as nieces and nephews, which would indicate he had siblings, but I have never heard of any. He had another wife, Margaret Byers Risenger, born September 17, 1880. They were married "June or May 1962," according to Sadie, and she died December 12, 1964. I remember that my parents were upset that he remarried "at his age!" (He was eighty-two). Actually, he and his housekeeper lived together after that. I don't remember my folks ever talking about that relationship.

The only memory I have of discussing my grandparents' health was when I was about five years old, sitting at the dinner table, talking about going to Orlando for the Christmas holidays. My mother looked at me sadly and said, "You know, this may be Grandma's last year!" And so we went to Florida the day after Christmas, for two weeks. And every year my mother told us it might be "Grandma's last year," and every year we went to Florida the day after Christmas, until I went away to college. Grandma died when I was a junior. I was in the Northwestern University infirmary with pneumonia at the time, so I couldn't go to the funeral anyway.

Aunt Sadie was born April 5, 1883, reared in Waite Hill, and taught school in Cleveland and Indianapolis. She retired in 1945 and moved to Orlando, Florida, living on one side of a duplex with my grandparents. Her middle name was Frances. Was that whom my father was named after? His original name was Robert Francis Grover (he later changed it to Frank).

Grandpa, Grandma, and Auntie were quiet and serious. Once in a while, I remember my grandfather chuckling to himself over some humorous joke he had just told. Grandma would smile. And that was about it. They were always telling my brother and me to shhh because grandma was sleeping. We played jacks or hopscotch on the driveway. Or we took our neighbor Victor over to nearby Lake Eola to feed the swans. I always hoped the only black swan would be there.

One of Auntie's friends sent her a postcard: "I am so glad to hear you have a full social life in Orlando, and that you are adapting so well …" Many of her pictures have her girlfriends in them. I was surprised to see a picture of her when she was young. She was pretty, with soft brown eyes and hair and a pleasant smile. She stayed single all her life.

The one memory I have of Auntie is that when she would visit, she'd bring her cloth-covered darning tool, slip my father's sock over the tool, and darn the holes in his sock. It was a good thing because my mother didn't darn or sew. Neither did I. If there was a hole in the sock, I just threw it away and bought a new one.

Auntie died November 15, 1968, and was buried at Mentor, Ohio, with the rest of the family. I am so grateful for the things she left for me.

SADIE'S LEGACY OF RESILIENCE

Certainly Great-Aunt Sadie's family had adventures, which her grandmother Lydia E. Freeman documents in her typewritten diary from the 1750s to the 1890s. Sadie's great-grandparents, Samuel and Sarah Freeman, and their ten kids headed out in a wagon from Massachusetts to Ohio, which is where the Hooses, Freemans, and eventually the Grovers resided. From Sadie's grandmother's diary:

> *To my dear daughter, Lydia Elizabeth*
>
> *When I promised you, recently, that I would write some sketches of the Freeman family for your perusal and if you see fit, to transmit them to your posterity, I did not well consider the infirmities of my age. As you have assumed for yourself and posterity another name, it is not unlikely that you will feel less interested in the history from which you come.*
>
> *I can trace the genealogy of the Freeman family back but a few generations. What information I have I received from my father.*
>
> *Samuel Freeman, who was my father's grandfather, lived in Sturbridge, Mass., and died there, but at what time I am not informed. He was a blacksmith by trade. He had five sons and four daughters, to wit:*
>
> *Benjamin*
> *Comfort*
> *Jared*
> *Samuel*
> *Walter (not sure if it is right)*
> *Rachel*
> *Martha*
> *Mary*
> *Ruth*

Most of them lived in or near the town of Sturbridge, Mass., Worcester Co.

Comfort was my grandfather. I have a distinct remembrance of seeing him in his last sickness. I was about 3 yrs. old. Though his education was meager, he possessed a good share of moral excellence. He was a blacksmith and by his anvil acquired a good estate. He lived on what is called "The Freeman Farm," in the south part of Sturbridge.

Comfort Freeman was born August 23, 1750. He married Lucy Walker, May 6, 1771. She was born Feb. 13, 1749. To them were born the following children, to wit:

Samuel
Clarinda
Sophia
Pliny
Lucy
Cynthia
Comfort
Augusta

He died Dec. 1806, aged 55¼ yrs.
She died Aug. 5, 1838, aged 83½ yrs.

Samuel was my father. I will inform you concerning his family later in tabular form.

My father had a vigorous mind and a good physical constitution. His education was above mediocrity for the time in which he lived. He was for many years a surveyor of land. He represented the town of Sturbridge in her legislature several times and was justice of the peace for the county of Worcester and was often called to other honors and responsible positions.

From the death of his father until he came to Ohio, he lived on "The Freeman Farm."

He married Sally (Sarah) Belknap, daughter of Peter Belknap of Sturbridge, on Oct. 10, 1799.

Their constantly increasing family made their lives very arduous, and it was often difficult to make "strap and buckle meet." Soon after the birth of their thirteenth child, my father made arrangements to remove with most of his large family to the state of Ohio.

Such were the facilities for journeying at that time (1825) that comparatively few undertook the performance. My oldest brother and two oldest sisters remained in the east until we had located our home in the wilds of Ohio.

Our journey was long, arduous, and tedious. Late in the evening of a Saturday night, the teams which brought us from Cleveland stopped at a log cabin called "Fay's Inn." Father, mother, and ten children with a hired man nearly filled the inn.

Weary and worn, our first need was rest. Our kind hostess inquired of mother the number of her children present, and on being told that it was ten, began to count and found only nine. Sure enough. One was missing. Had she fallen into some of the bottomless mud holes which we had just passed through?

She (Clarinda) was finally found fast asleep in the wagon.

The township of "Parma," then called "Greenbrier," was then nearly an unbroken wilderness. A few families had settled several years before on the road that is now the turnpike and a few in the southeast corner of the township. The road through the township was truly horrible—until after our arrival there, there had been no schools and no religious meetings in that place.

Many interesting events which occurred during a year or two of our residence in "Greenbrier" might be mentioned but I pass them.

Cleveland, which then was our base of supplies, was at that time only a village of a few hundred inhabitants.

In case of sickness, no doctor could be found nearer than that place.

This was the day of "small things," which can hardly be realized in this day of railroads, telegraphs, phonographs, etc.

NEWSPAPER ARTICLES FROM AUNT SADIE

Era of Neighborhood Store Will Be Remembered

In this modern day of the brightly lighted, mammouth supermarkets with frozen, canned and packaged foods stocked ceiling high on uniform racks and in frosty coolers, it is sadly noted that Arthur H. Hoose, 80, retired Painesville grocer, died last week.

For 40 years he operated Hoose's Market at Grant Street and Mentor Avenue. During those 40 years, it seemed as if nothing ever changed inside the old-fashioned store.

It was here that neighborhood children, clutching a few copper pennies, experienced the thrill of making their first purchase. Naturally it was candy and generally those sugar-covered green spearmint leaves or a roll of bubble gum. Many youngsters enroute to school would stop to buy a writing tablet, pencils and erasers.

The tall, bespeckled, blond man with the serious face, gave his young customers the same efficient service he gave adult shoppers.

In the 40 years Mr. Hoose was in business, nothing ever seemed to change. The smell of spices was always evident, the candy case never moved its position, the same sweets were on the same shelves. Behind the meat counter and around the chopping block, sawdust always was scattered on the floor.

Mr. Hoose retired in 1958 from the grocery business. Yet his oldtime customers will never forget his store and the way he operated. They will always have pleasant memories of his independent neighborhood market of yesteryear.

...rs. Nellie Gunn, 82, Dies At Home

Mrs. Nellie E. Gunn, 82, died at midnight at her home at 88 Washington St., where she had been ill for several months.

She was a member of the First Church, Congregational, and belonged to its Women's association. She had resided in this city for 29 years.

She is survived by her husband, Edgar C. Gunn; one daughter, Mrs. M. B. Chase, Mentor; 10 grandchildren and two great grandchildren.

Friends may call at the Nixon Funeral home, beginning Thursday night, where services will be held Friday at 2 p. m. The Rev. Arthur C. Decker will officiate. Burial will follow in the family lot in Mentor.

A. H. Hoose, Grocer, Dies

Arthur H. Hoose, 83, of 660 Mentor Ave., died Tuesday night in Lake County Memorial Hospital after suffering a cerebral stroke.

Mr. Hoose had been born July 13, 1877 at Waite Hill and had come to Painesville in 1918. He married the former Flora Reed of Huntsburg in 1896. She preceeded him in death in 1955.

Mr. Hoose had owned and operated a grocery store in Painesville for 40 years and had retired in 1958.

Survivors include his two sons, Dr. Kenneth A. Hoose of Kent; Sterling R. Hoose of Cleveland Heights, and four grandchildren.

Funeral services will be held Friday at 3 p.m. at the Spear Funeral Home, where friends may call from 7 to 9 p.m. Thursday. Rev. Glen M. Warner of the Methodist Church will officiate. Burial will be in Mentor Cemetery.

Clipping from an old newspaper.

Mrs. Wells of Union St. Willoughby, Ohio, favors us with a clipping from an old newspaper which she came across at her home recently.

WAITE HILL MAN SHOWS CORN HUSKING ABILITY IN 1879. 1879.

George Hoose of Waite Hill , on Nov. 10, 1879, husked 122 bu. of corn inside of ten hours. Took the shocks down, husked them, tied up the shocks and set them up as fastas they were husked.
Didn't do it on a wager but just for recreation. He didn't charge 10 cents admission to spectators or advertise that he would give anyone ten bushels start and catch up with him before night; but if anyone has done better than that he would like to know it, so that he can try again some day when he means business.
(Signed) A Waite Hiller

The item further remarks that George husked 57 shocks, 42 hills in a shock. (2094)
Tuesday, the 11 th. Warren Hoose husked 43 shocks with 64 hills in a shock(2702)

GEORGE G. HOOSE MARRIES
LYDIA ELIZABETH FREEMAN

George H. Hoose, born June 28, 1854, has married Lydia Elizabeth Freeman, born August 31, 1853. Mr. Hoose is one of the foremost farmers in the area. They were married on August 8, 1878.

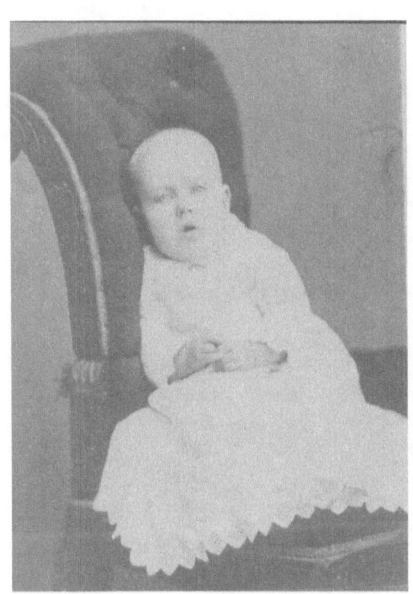
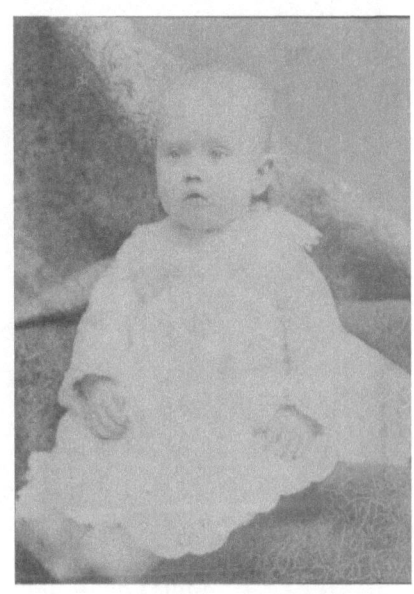

Ruth Freeman Hoose
Born May 24, 1880
Willoughby, Ohio

Sadie Frances Hoose
Born April 5, 1883
Willoughby, Ohio

Ruth's doll—pink dress and blue eyes

Sadie's doll—blue dress and brown eyes

Dolls have the china heads, leather hands, and cloth bodies typical of dolls in the 1880s.

PARIAN DOLLS

Doll belonging to Ruth Freeman Hoose (my grandmother), 1880
Pink dress, blue eyes, kid hands darkened by oily fingers holding them

The word "parian" is defined as fine, unglazed bisque that resembles the white marble found on the Greek island of Paros. Paros is one of the Cyclades island group located in the Aegean Sea southeast of Athens. Author Janet Johl provides the following information in her 1946 book *More About Dolls:* "The marble was hewn from the subterranean quarries of Paros for Praxiteles and his fellow sculptors. Thus, our Parian dolls of the 19th Century take us back to the 6th Century BC, to the teeming life of one of the most artistic periods in human history."

In the 1995 *UFDC List of Accepted Terms*, we find these dolls defined as follows: "Parian doll: doll made of fine white bisque (unglazed porcelain) without tinting. The features, hair and cheeks may be painted. Occasionally, these dolls have glass eyes."

My great-aunt Sadie Frances Hoose's doll, 1883
Blue dress, brown eyes

DOILIES

A doily is an ornamental mat, originally the name of a fabric, from *Doily*, a seventeenth-century London draper.[1] Doilies are usually made of cotton or linen thread, often crocheted but may also be knitted. Openwork allows the underlying surface to show through. In addition to their decorative function, doilies have the utilitarian role of protecting wood furniture from scratches caused by crockery or decorative objects.

Many patterns for crocheting or knitting doilies were published by thread manufacturers in the first part of the twentieth century. The designs could be circular or oval and started from the center and worked outward, reminiscent of the polar coordinate system. Doilies may be made by crocheting rows on a grid pattern using a technique called filet crochet, similar to points on the Cartesian coordinate system.

1. "doily." From Wikipedia, the free encyclopedia

Here is my great-aunt Sadie F. Hoose with Jimmy and me on Christmas 1943. I am wearing my little blue dress with the Polly Flinders hand smocking across the top, and Jimmy is wearing matching blue. Auntie doesn't smile in any of the pictures, but here she looks like she might be getting ready to smile. Interesting since she is the one who said, "Smile and the whole world smiles with you." I am laughing, however. I always do what I am told.

This is where Grandma Ruth Freeman and Grandpa Harry Lewis Grover lived, at 312 East Yale Avenue, Orlando, Florida. Our great-aunt Sadie Frances Hoose lived at 314 East Yale Avenue, on the left side of the duplex. When we would go to Florida to visit Grandma and Grandpa, Auntie would stay with friends, and we would stay at her place. We'd spend one week with them, and one week touring Florida. I remember being told that Grandma was too sick to have us be there for two weeks. And when we were there, we had to be very quiet. I played jacks on the driveway. And Jimmy and I played with Victor, the neighbor.

GROVERS

GRANDSON OF LOCAL WOMAN GETS THE
ALPHA TAU OMEGA WM. HART MEDAL

Friends of Mr. Harry L. Grover and Mrs. Grover (Ruth Hoose) of Indianapolis, Indiana, are glad to know that their son, Robert, has been awarded the "Wm. Hart Medal" by the A.T.O. Fraternity of which he is a member, for receiving all As, the highest grade received in the freshman class. He also has the highest grade given to any student at the Purdue University, Lafayette, Indiana. He is a grandson of Mrs. Lillie E. Hoose, formerly of Mentor, and also of Mrs. Mary Grover. Graduated with highest honors in Civil Engineering—1926.

This handwritten copy of a newspaper article was in my Aunt Sadie's diary, which she gave to me at the time of her death. There is no mention of what newspaper it was in or the date it was printed. Since she is mentioned in the headline, I knew it was from Grandma's hometown. I have a picture of Dad, but there is no date on it, so I'm not sure if it is high school or college. It is the only picture I have of him from his youth.

The only memory I have of my father from this time in his life is his many comments about how he *always worked* during the Depression years and always supported his family. Once he even did construction work (probably the only Phi Beta Kappa worker on that road). It gives me a sense of the high value he placed on work and also on taking care of and providing for his family, something he always did throughout his lifetime until he died.

MY MOTHER'S WEDDING

The time is 2:25 PM according to the grandfather clock. It is June 25, 1927, the day that my mother married my father, Robert F. Grover, in Indianapolis, Indiana. A hula girl lamp on top of a table runner decorates the table sitting at her side. They tell me that the five-to-six-inch fringe around the bottom of the lampshade represents the grass skirt that the hula girl wears.

Right in the center of the picture stands the bride, my mother, Helen Louise Hanks. She is only eighteen years old. She looks serene, at peace in her light-colored wedding dress, which falls into scalloped edges just below her knees. Her bountiful hat is equal in size to the face of the grandfather clock. It sits stylishly to one side, with a bow in the back. She smiles slightly, her eyes look straight ahead, and her hair falls in soft curls just below her ears, a style often seen in the twenties. She wears a triple strand of pearls and carries a bouquet of flowers so large they cover her body from one side to the other. She wears satin heels, and I believe this is the only picture where I have seen her wearing such attractive three-inch heels. She later had a history of bad feet and could not tolerate the pain.

How I wish I had more pictures! Where is her father? Did he give her away? Where was the wedding, reception, and honeymoon? My father often said, "I picked your mother right up out of the streets and put shoes on her feet." Did he mean this? She used to laugh, but she never denied it. Was her family that poor? The grandfather clock and the big hula girl lamp don't seem to be possessions of the down and out.

My mother never talked to me of her courtship, wedding, or early marriage. I have a vague memory of her saying that Aunt Helen went with them on their honeymoon and slept at the foot of their bed, which in retrospect seems absurd. And my father alluded to the fact that my mother was naive in every way. I so wish I had asked more questions!

The next time my parents show up is in the 1939 Aurora telephone directory, where he is listed as an engineer at Love Bros., Inc., and they live at 18 South Elmwood Drive, which would be my first home.

THE SOUTHERN BELLE

"I'm going daaaawntown in a little bit. Do you want to go with me?" My mother told us she was raised in the Saaaauth, and that was how she talked, with a drawl and an accent. My father was also from the South, but he did not have any accent.

Mother was "five feet two, with eyes of blue," something I wanted to be (I was much taller and towered over her). She had brown hair, turning slightly gray around the edges, but was a young-looking thirty-five years when I was born. I looked at the home movies from that era, learning more about my family. My mother walked the baby carriage in heels, dress, and a fancy hat, wearing a skirt and blouse. Because it was 1940 and the camera was probably one of the first Kodak movie cameras, the film was black and white. However, throughout all of the movies, my mother wore dresses and hats—different ones each time. The hat in this picture was turban-like. In another one, she had a small black hat with a bright red plume that was about eight inches tall. Smiling, sometimes turning away from the camera and looking shy, she swooshed her hand at us as if to say, "You don't really want to take my picture." And she instructed me never to leave the house in the morning without looking presentable, whatever that meant. Perhaps to always be ready in case someone caught me "in the movies."

My mother said she was prejudiced because of where she was raised. Many times I heard the story of how I invited a "little colored girl" to share my dressing room at the YWCA when I was a child. I think she didn't know what to do.

The thing I found so interesting when my mother told us how she was raised in the "Saaaauth" was that she came from Indianapolis, Indiana. Am I the only one who never considered that the "South"?

AURORA CITY DIRECTORIES

1929: No listing for Robert F. or Helen L. Grover

1931: No listing for Robert F. or Helen L. Grover

1936: No listing for Robert F. or Helen L. Grover

1939: Grover, Robert F. (Helen) engineer, Love Bros., Inc.
    residence: 18 S. Elmwood Drive

    Oldham, William F. (Helen L.) residence: 785 Gleason Ave.

1941: Grover, Robert F. (Helen L.) sales manager-engineer, Love Bros., Inc.
    residence: 18 S. Elmwood Drive

1943: Grover, Robert F. (Helen L.) sales manager, Love Bros., Inc.
    residence: 206 Gladstone Ave.

1946: Grover, Robert F. (Helen) sales manager, Love Bros., Inc.
    residence: 1026 Downer Pl.

1948: same as 1946 listing

1952: Grover, Robert F. (Helen L.) President, Love Bros., Inc.
    residence: 1026 Downer Pl. Tel 2-4017

1954: same as 1952 listing

1955: same as 1952 listing

1956: same as 1952 listing

LOVE BROTHERS INC.

Following a brief ceremony on Thursday, May 25, 2006, the former Baje-Steere foundry, one of the largest vacant buildings downtown, is being demolished. The building, part of a 27-acre riverfront site, will be imploded gradually and then cleared and cleaned over a period of two years. Polluted soil, an electrical substation, and the former Burlington Depot all provide challenges to the future development of the site. The plan is for offices, shops, and 1,000 residences to be built.

Originally named Love Brothers Inc., the foundry opened in Aurora in 1882 and was one of many large manufacturing sites that made Aurora prosperous for much of the 20th century. At the peak of the Industrial Age, it created the area's real wealth, its jobs, and the building blocks of the city. The building remaining today was the tallest and last built, in 1919.

Love Brothers poured iron and steel into massive beams that held up most buildings across the Midwest. There were smaller products, such as most of the manhole covers in Aurora's streets, and even the huge park-size swing set in our backyard.*

My dad moved up the ranks at Love Brothers: engineer, salesman, sales manager, vice president, president. I used to work there during summer vacations when he served as president of the company. I learned about class distinctions, but at that time, I didn't know what they were. The other "girls" who worked in the foundry were close, but when I walked into the room, they all hushed up fast. I never quite felt as if I belonged, and I never quite knew why.

I can remember when he took me into the foundry to view the smudge-faced men bustling around cauldrons of molten metal. They were pouring metal in great showers of sparks.

In the latter half of the twentieth century, its vitality declined, along with much of America's heavy industry. The foundry was sold multiple times, with Baje-Steere being the last own before going out of business in the late 1980s.

I feel proud that we were associated with such an important industry in the city of Aurora, and my father certainly appears to have been extremely successful in that industry.

I found the article about the death of Joy Love, the founder of Love Brothers, Inc., at the Aurora Historical Museum.

*From "Baje-Steere Comes Down," by David Garbe, *Beacon News*, Friday, May 26, 2006.

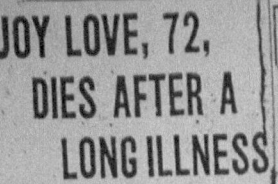

JOY LOVE, 72, DIES AFTER A LONG ILLNESS

Survives Three Major Operations Only to Succumb to Attack of Bronchitis.

WAS A LEADER IN INDUSTRY

Joy Love
Oct. 28, 1856.   Jan. 8, 1929.

Joy Love, above, born in Aurora 72 years ago last October and one of the best known manufacturers in the state, died at his home in Downer Place yesterday afternoon.

Joy Love, 72, president of Love Brothers, Inc., and the Aurora Foundry company and one of the oldest native born residents of Aurora, died yesterday afternoon at 3:45 o'clock at his home, 545 Downer Place.

One of the industrial leaders of the state, Mr. Love was also one of its best liked of men. The friendly person, he never was so beset with business care he did not have the good word. A noted story teller and wit, his company was always eagerly sought. In his society men or women or children found cheer.

Joy Love's part in building Aurora was notable. For many years he was the employer of hundreds of men at good wages and any public endeavor found in him a willing and liberal giver of means and time. The very fact that a small foundry he and his brother John established almost a half century ago was developed into an important iron and steel works with a large foundry as a subsidiary firm, tells in itself that he made large contribution to the growth and prosperity of his home town. The good wages he paid, his friendliness and wit, his love of the outdoors and regard for people generally, made him invaluable citizen and intrenched him in the affections of his fellows.

Aurora would be indeed unfortunate if it were to have no more Joy Loves. They are the men who make for more kindly feeling and happiness. They not only develop the community, industrially and as home site. They enrich its social life for years and years to come.

FAMILY HONORS
WCC graduates credit support
from parents, siblings.
VOICE, D1

HIGH SCHOOL BASEBALL REGIONALS
WVHS REACHES TITLE GAME
Mike Wonz hits four doubles, leads Warriors to 10-2 win over Marmion. SPORTS, B1

OUR VIEW
There's too much drama
over the drive-in
VIEWPOINT, D2

The BeaconNews

THE VOICE OF THE FOX VALLEY SINCE 1846 • WWW.SUBURBANCHICAGONEWS.COM • AURORA, ILLINOIS

FRIDAY, MAY 26, 2006
50 CENTS

OLD FOUNDRY MAKING WAY FOR NEW FACE OF DOWNTOWN

PHOTOS BY DONNELL COLLINS / STAFF PHOTOGRAPHER

Aurora Mayor Tom Weisner spray paints his sentiments for his wife, Marilyn, on the side of the former Baje-Steere foundry just before the start of demolition at the old manufacturing facility in downtown Aurora Thursday afternoon.

Baje-Steere comes down

By David Garbe
STAFF WRITER

AURORA — Taking the first step in a multi-year downtown re-development project, Geneva-based Sho-Deen Inc. began Thursday to demolish the former Baje-Steere foundry.

The foundry has sat vacant for more than a decade on a riverfront site that Sho-Deen hopes to transform into a complex of high-rise residential, retail and office buildings in downtown Aurora.

Over the next few days, the building will be imploded gradually, said Pat Browne, the project manager. Workers will spend many months clearing the site of debris and contamination. Cleaning the entire 27-acre site is expected to take two years.

The process began Thursday with a brief ceremony that drew dozens of community and business leaders to gather in the cavernous building for one last glimpse of what once had been a thriving workshop.

Amid the rusty, twisted metal fixtures and age-blackened windows, even the most enthusiastic proponents of the redevelopment found themselves pausing in their celebrations to reflect on what the building once represented.

Originally named Love Brothers

✦ *Turn to* **BAJE-STEERE, A2**

A backhoe begins tearing down the walls of the old foundry to make way for a major redevelopment by Geneva developer Sho-Deen Inc. Entire site cleanup at the former metalworking facility is expected to take up to two years.

Possible for site

Although Sho-Deen Inc. has not yet developed a specific plan
for its 27-acre site on the east bank of the Fox River in downtown Aurora, the company's agreement with the city allows for
a range of potential buildings:

- 1,000 townhomes, condominiums and apartments
- 125,000 square feet of commercial, retail and office space
- Public parking deck
- Hotel/conference center
- Pedestrian bridge
- Metra train station

The total cost of the project is expected to be $200 million.

BAJE-STEERE

From page A1

Inc., the foundry was one of many large manufacturing sites that made Aurora prosperous for much of the 20th century.

Back then, at the apex of the Industrial Age, it was the kind of place that created the area's real wealth — not to mention its jobs and the very building blocks of the city.

Love Brothers poured iron and steel into massive beams that would hold up buildings across the Midwest. There were smaller products, too: most of the manhole covers in Aurora's streets once bore the Love Brothers imprint.

Among the business and community leaders who gathered Thursday to watch the building's demise, most could remember the days when the site still was home to smudge-faced men bustling around cauldrons of molten metal.

"My grandfather worked here more than 50 years ago," said Wally Mundy. When Mundy was a child, his grandmother would bring him to visit the foundry. "I remember when the doors would open and you could see them pouring" metal in great showers of sparks, the Aurora business-man said.

The foundry opened in Aurora in 1882 and grew to be a sprawl-ing complex of buildings. The building that remains today was the tallest and the last to be built, in 1919.

In the later half of the 20th century, the vitality of the found-ry declined along with much of America's heavy industry, which spent decades consolidating, au-tomating and eventually relocat-ing to the developing world,

The foundry was sold multiple times, with Baje-Steere being the last owner to put its name on the roof before going out of busi-ness in the late 1980s.

"This does represent the past and we have a proud past. But we also have a brilliant future," said Aurora Mayor Tom Weisner at Thursday's demolition ceremo-ny. "The sense of loss or senti-mentality is certainly overshadowed by a sense of joy."

Weisner praised Sho-Deen for investing in a property that, de-spite its prime riverfront loca-tion, features "every imaginable form of environmental prob-lem."

Now that clean-up is under way, the next challenge for the redevelopment is finding a way to re-locate a ComEd electrical substation and network of power lines that crisscross the site.

That task has not yet begun, Sho-Deen executives said. The company is in the process of re-viewing concept plans for the site from several architects.

*The old Love Brothers foundry, where my father, Robert
F. Grover, was president. It was located near the Chicago,
Burlington and Quincy Railroad, where my grandfather
William Hanks worked as a carpenter from 1905 to 1906.*

AURORA

Many of my relatives lived in Aurora: William and Emma, Bonnie Guy and Vida, Roy and Harriett, Robert and Helen Grover, and my brother, Jim, and myself.

Aurora is the Roman name for Eos, the Greek goddess of the dawn. Eos was the name of our West Aurora High School yearbook in the 1950s. When a post office was established here, the first name chosen was Waubonsie, after the Potawatomi chief; however, there was already a post office by that name in Illinois. Many local settlers were from New York State, and it is said that the town was named for East Aurora, New York. Other nearby towns, such as Batavia, Oswego, and Montgomery, also bear New York State names. Another theory is that "Aurora" was adopted because it is a transliteration of Waubonsie, which means "early dawn."

Some great facts from the historical society Web site include the fact that Aurora is the birthplace of the Burlington Railroad, where my maternal great-grandfather was first employed. He moved to Aurora from the East Coast.

Aurora is called "The City of Lights." In 1881, Aurora was the first city in the Midwest to adopt electricity for street lighting. This was accomplished by mounting powerful arc lamps atop 150-foot towers scattered throughout town. Five years later, Aurora became the first city in the world to own and operate a municipal electric power plant.

By 1908, the towers were gone, but hundreds of lower-level lights were in place. Then the local merchants funded a new decorative lighting system in the downtown area. At that time, Aurora officially adopted the slogan "The City of Lights."

McCarty Mills - In 1834, brothers Joseph and Samuel McCarty came west from upstate New York to seek their fortunes. They built a sawmill and a gristmill on the Fox River. In 1837, a post office was established, and the village became Aurora.

Prehistoric Creatures - Over ten thousand years ago, mastodons, ancestors of the elephant, roamed the Fox Valley area. In 1934, while digging a lake at Phillips Park, dozens of mastodon bones were discovered and given to the Aurora Historical Society.

Native Americans - For thousands of years, Native Americans inhabited the Fox River Valley. Just prior to the coming of the white man, Potawatomi Chief Waubonsie had his village there. In 1835, Waubonsie and his people were relocated west of the Mississippi River.

East Side, West Side - Aurora began as two separate villages on either side of the Fox River. In 1857, the two were united as the city of Aurora.

First Public School District - East Aurora (District 131), established in 1851, was the first free public school district in Illinois, two years before the statewide establishment of a public school system.

Champions of the World - The Aurora Zouaves, a military close-order drill team, was formed in 1887. By 1896, wins in successive competitions earned them the tile "Champions of the World." From 1897 to 1906, the Aurora Zouaves were famous the world over. The team toured with Buffalo Bill's Wild West Show and with Forepaugh & Sells Brothers Circus. The Zouaves also toured Europe on their own in 1901–02, playing before thousands of spectators and the crown heads of Europe. I have pictures of Grandpa Bonnie Guy and his brother Roy in their Zouave hats and tassels.

Oldest Sports Rivalry - The longest-standing sports rivalry in the state of Illinois is between East and West Aurora high schools. The schools have played an annual football contest, usually on Thanksgiving Day, since 1893; basketball has been played between the two since 1912.

Corset Center of the World - A century ago, Aurora was the center of a thriving industry in female support garments, with three major corset factories locating here between the 1880s and 1910s. The earliest, the Chicago Corset Company, was the second largest in the world; in 1890, the company employed six hundred young women and girls, producing two million corsets annually.

Early Flight - The first public flight demonstration took place at the Driving Park in Aurora, when a Wright brothers' plane did demonstrations for the city's 1910 Fourth of July celebration.

World Center for Steel Cabinetry - From the 1900s to the 1920s, several manufacturers of steel lockers, shelving, desks, and cabinets located in Aurora. These included Lyon Metal (whose employee assistance program we created and continue to manage today), Aurora Metal, All-Steel, Durabilt, and Equipto.

For more information, contact http://www.aurorahistoricalsociety. org/factiods.html

PATSY:
BIRTH–EIGHTEEN YEARS

ANTIQUE CAMERAS

I always thought my father, Robert F. Grover, bought the first movie camera and took pictures of every important event in my brother's and my life, from 1940 until 1953. I have all the movies and have had nearly one hundred still pictures made from them, to replace the pictures that were lost in the flood of 1973. I found some information about this camera from a calendar for 1940. It states that the "Cine-Kodak Eight Model 20 movie camera retails for $29.95." This was probably a lot of money in 1940, but I just knew my father would have one of the first movie cameras made! He always got the first of everything.

I also have an antique Brownie Hawkeye camera, which I used all through grade school. It produced the little three-by-three-inch pictures that I still have. Memories of Quarryledge Camp, Freeman Grade School, and many of my grade school friends are from the fifties and my little camera.

HELLO, WORLD! HERE I COME!

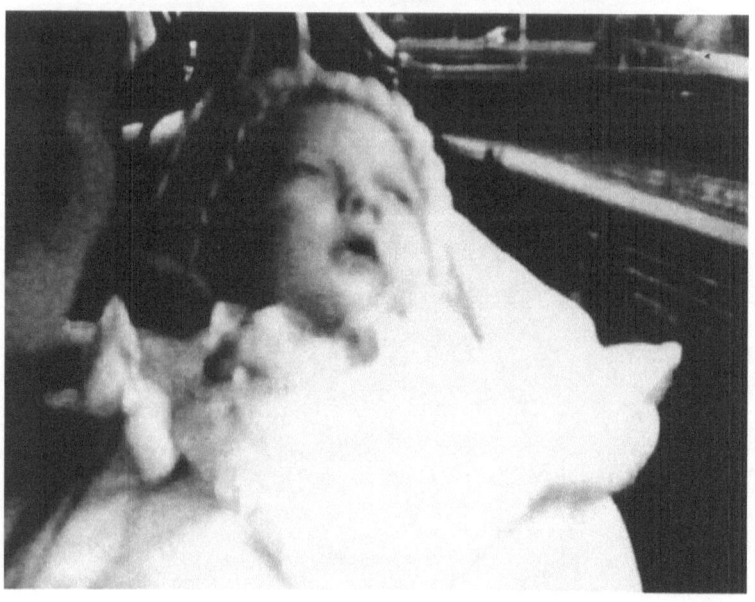

"Okay, Helen, is it Barb … or is it Pat? I'm not letting you get out of the car until we choose a name, if it's a girl," my father said.

"Bob, I have to go into the hospital. I think I'm having labor pains!"

"Then pick a name and you're welcome to go on in."

"All right, then. Patricia Ann Grover is what it is."

I heard that story so many times, about how I was named before mom went into Aurora's Copley Hospital and Dr. Heimdal delivered me. My parents had been married for thirteen years and had not conceived. They had the adoption papers completed in January, when they found out they were pregnant.

In those days, women went under anesthesia and they stayed in the hospital for two weeks. So although I was born on August 2, 1940,

I met my "oldest friend," JudyMeyers, born on July 27. She and her mother were our next-door neighbors in the hospital.

Mom and Dad brought me home to my first house at 18 South Elmwood Drive in Aurora. In 1943, we moved to 206 Gladstone Avenue, and my father became a sales manager at Love Bros. My brother was born that year.

As I look at the movies, I realize there were many people at my house when I came home from the hospital: Grandma and Grandpa Grover, a nurse, a young girl, and another woman I don't know. Surely my mother didn't have that many people helping to take care of me!

My coming-home-from-the-hospital outfit was a pink hat and coat. I have my mother's blue eyes and "rosebud lips." She is proud of those small pointed lips. I look healthy, with full cheeks and a round face.

I wonder what my family dreamed of for me. To follow in their footsteps? To strike out and follow my own dreams and passions? Girls were somewhat limited in the forties and fifties, but those limits began to expand during my lifetime, allowing me to grow and change with and beyond the times.

MY EARLIEST MEMORY

I never know for sure if my earliest memory is really a memory or simply the result of watching our family movies so many times.

I have a vague recollection of the feeling of one of the icicles on the Christmas tree when I was two or three years old. It just brushed my face. In the movie, I pushed it away. This brings back all the times I helped decorate the tree and my father insisted that we put on the icicles one at a time. The Christmas tree always looked big and beautiful, and the icicles were perfect. This was how we did everything in my life: perfectly.

I also look at the movies of Christmas Day when I was about two years old. I was the "star." I remember my father had big floodlights set up in the living room. I came walking down the stairs, my long blond banana curls arranged perfectly on my shoulders, wearing a little short-sleeved white blouse and a little blue jumper. I walked slowly. I was supposed to be seeing my gifts for the first time. I was obviously being coached by someone (these are silent movies) and "posed" with my new toys.

The pictures that haunt me and bring tears to my eyes are these Christmas pictures where my eyes are red, and I have a sad, faraway look in them. Looking at this little girl grabs my heart and makes me feel compassion for her. I have been told I had "pinkeye," but the only other time I had conjunctivitis (pinkeye) was when I was in the process of losing my job, was extremely stressed, and was working hard to keep my feelings hidden. Did I first learn this at age two? And why was I so stressed on Christmas morning?

A MOTHER'S DREAM

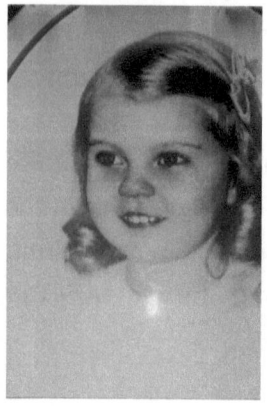  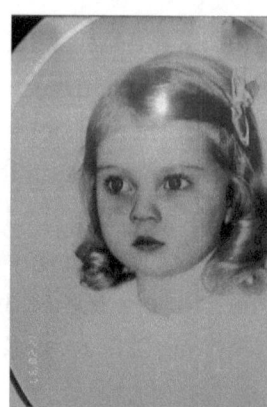

May 26, 2002

Dear Mom,

"It's a girl!" I never knew what these words conjured up for you—I never thought to ask. You had been waiting thirteen years to have a child, had visited an adoption agency, and now you had me. I know that when *I* heard those words, I was so excited. My son was two, and now I would have my daughter. What more could I ask?

I remember some of the struggles of growing up in the forties and fifties because you and I were different. I know now that I was more like my father, and I suspect that was difficult for you. I also know now that you lived a lot of your life vicariously through me. Your mother had died when you were eleven, and you got married very young, the month after you graduated high school. So you began your dreams for me: to be popular, to be a cheerleader, to be prom or homecoming queen. I tried my best to please you and believe I did well. I still remember the night I was crowned prom queen. You were in the front row of the balcony in the high school gymnasium and nearly fell over onto the floor when they announced my name.

I remember saying later, "They really should have given the crown to my mother because she worked much harder and wanted it much more than I did!"

I knew I had to go to college. But I also knew I had to get married. I married the man *you* wanted me to, rather than the person I met my senior year, whom I brought home to meet you and Dad. I remember you saying that the boy you chose would be "more successful and provide for me better." I followed your advice. I have often wondered, however, now that we are divorced, what could have happened if I had followed my own instincts.

You became a victim of the medical system in the seventies, a system that labeled menopause as a serious mental disease, and you were so medicated and depressed that I hardly knew you. Between the pills and the drinking, your personality changed completely. When Dad died in the early seventies, you had become so dependent and helpless that you couldn't—didn't even want to—take care of yourself. I remember being so angry with you for that. By then, I was raising my two children as a single parent and working full time. I tried having you live with me; I was going to make you independent. But that failed, and you went back to your assisted, medicated living. I felt terrible.

In the late seventies, I completed my master's degree in social work and was beginning to launch my midlife career. Every time we got together, you would carefully point out all the reasons I should be getting married rather than starting a career. I still remember the day I was putting up screens in my kitchen and you said, "Now, honey, if you just had a husband, he could do that for you." I remember feeling annoyed as I reminded you, "I put up the screens all during my married life."

One of my most poignant memories was Thanksgiving weekend of 1982. My son, daughter, and I had spent weeks rejuvenating the old house that would become my office for my own private group practice. My son built the big sign in the front yard: PAPE & ASSOC. I hung the special artwork you had given me of a country scene near Aurora, painted by a friend of yours. It was hanging right over my desk in my therapy office. I picked you up at the nursing home and brought you over to show you this place that was my pride and joy. I later realized that you had no idea of the significance of this event for me when you looked into my eyes, with love and sadness, and said, "Oh, honey, it's just too bad that you could not find a good man!" Those were your last significant words to me. You died the next day. *Your* dream for me never came true.

My daughter is now grown and is also a licensed clinical social worker. I too had a dream for her. My dream was that she would branch out, get some independent experience, and then return to Chicago, eventually taking over the business that I started twenty years ago. She did the first half: went to California and got a job. She also met a man, got married, and had two beautiful boys. And I realize now that she is never returning to Chicago.

So we are two mothers, each of whom had a dream for her daughter, and neither of our dreams came true. And I am learning only now, as a mother of a grown daughter, just how *hard* it is to let go—and to encourage our loved ones to fulfill their own dreams, to trust their own instincts, and to soar.

A FAIRY TALE

Once upon a time, there was a little girl. Everyone said she had blond hair, but it looks like there is some red in it. And you know what they say about redheads: they get what they want. So you, Patsy, set out to see what you wanted. I love this part of the home movies because you look close to your daddy, with your cheek resting on his, and everyone sure said that couldn't be true. I know you thought your daddy would always take care of you, and you would never have to worry about anything. And he seemed to. He was successful, and he paid for all your lessons. You traveled—to Florida, New York, and California.

So what happened? Everyone says he began to drink too much. You used to sit on the stairs and listen to them fight. And then he would hit her. And that was your clue to run into the kitchen and get in between them. Or just sit quietly so you wouldn't realize how out of control and afraid you felt. Your mother began to drink. And then there was the Valium. Then your dad lost his job, and the family had to move to Milwaukee. You went to Northwestern University, and so you got out of some of it. But do you remember Isabel Parker telling you your mother tried to walk into Lake Michigan? And then when you were a sophomore, your father called you, crying, asking you to come home because he had to commit your mother into a mental hospital. And then you got married. Your husband abused you and then you began to drink more and more.

Wow! This isn't a fairy tale; it's a horror story where nobody learns from his or her experiences. As my spiritual director would say, "Where is God in all this?" Was she just watching and knowing in her astute wisdom, that I had to come to my own realizations? And how long would it take? My father died from cirrhosis of the liver; my mother moved back to Aurora, but this time into a nursing home; my brother disowned all of us, married, and moved to Milwaukee to become a teacher; and I continued to drink and not learn.

In 1972, I went to Lutheran General, although I chose to check out early and drank both weekends. The staff was worried about my safety. But while I was there, Janet and Ivan, AA volunteers, must have given me their business card. On September 22, 1972, I called

them and asked for help. It was a long road, but slowly I began to see that I wasn't crazy, and I could be healed through the Twelve Steps.

Could this be God's wisdom coming through? The 12-step program sure looked different from Young Life Christian Youth Group or church or anything I had learned to date. But it worked, and I kept healing.

Did I live "happily ever after"? No way. What did I learn? Perhaps simply to stay open to possibility. And that the answer to my question "And where is God in all this?" is "Right here within me."

A REWRITTEN FAIRY TALE

There was once a woman who gave herself permission to accept her gifts, rewrite her life story, and be successful according to *her* definition of success. She "let her hair down" and accepted her own feelings and fun. She began to listen to and trust herself. She looked at her own visions. She held her own inner child, remembered—but *lightly*—her own childhood. Her own wonder child lived within, protected and safe. So did her Divine Feminine—*God She.* They loved each other, smiled, laughed, and played. She felt free to be herself, to be accepted by others, to be loved by her God, and to *experience* that love.

She explored the old myths. First was work hard and be perfect in order to be loved and to succeed. Success was being loved and feeling loved, especially by a man. Did anyone in my family really feel loved? I have decided that my alcoholism, which led me into therapy and AA, was a gift. It was my gift. It was the gift of love from my "dark side." There was *nothing* I could do to deserve it.

Another myth: never give up, even if it is abusive. My parents told me to marry the man who had abused me. My father was abusive. I have changed this myth in my adult life to this: Persevere but set limits and boundaries in order to protect yourself. Trust your own gut and listen to your inner wisdom. Be gentle with yourself.

One last message: If you're going to do something, do it right or don't do it at all. I have changed this message to this: It's okay to take risks and to do the best you can. The only time something is a mistake is when you don't learn from it. All mistakes are for learning.

All these behaviors are examples of the love and resilience that my ancestors demonstrated: persevere in spite of obstacles, be willing to look at yourself and change, and experience and express love.

THE OLDHAMS

Here is Aunt Geraldine, Uncle Marrian, Nancy, Jerry Jean, and Sue. These pictures are taken from my movies, and as I looked at the movies, I was struck with how much fun they seemed to be having as a family. Uncle Marrian was turning somersaults in the grass, and everyone was laughing. They lived in Dayton, and we did not see them very often. I wish I knew more about them. My cousin Sue is the one who sent me the pictures that began this project, and Nancy sent me some more pictures and information about Grandpa Bonnie Guy Hanks. Jerry Jean and Nancy are deceased.

Aunt Geraldine is lovely in all the pictures. She is stylish and attractive and looks as if she took good care of herself. I love this picture of Sue pushing me in one of the old strollers. There's my reddish hair again.

SLEDDING AT PHILLIPS PARK (1942–43)

I remember flying down the hills at Phillips Park like it was yesterday. Here we were, getting ready for a wonderful adventure. Dad held my hand, I dragged the sled, and we climbed up the hill. Then I sat in front of him on the sled. His legs wrapped around my small two-year-old body, his arms grabbed the rope so he could steer, and we edged forward on the hill. Suddenly, the sled took off. It seemed like we were going sixty miles an hour. The freezing air and snow forced me to close my eyes. My screams were not fear but delight. I felt so safe, nestled against my father's chest.

"Let's do it again!" I begged him.

"We have to go home now, honey, but we will come back again soon."

I knew that the promise he made was one that he would keep, so I looked forward to that in anticipation. Dragging the sled, we started the trek home, hand in hand.

"NO!"

I was two, on our vacation at Blaesings, Wisconsin, burrowing both my feet into the ground, folding my arms across my chest, scowling, and expressing my anger and frustration with a loud "No!" Watching our home movies was a favorite activity, and this particular scene always brought a comment from my mother. "There is Patsy," she would say with a laugh, "being stubborn and saying no!" It was obvious she was enjoying this moment, perhaps vicariously as she did so many things in my life, things she was too afraid to try.

No one but my father was allowed to express anger or aggression. This was in line with society in the forties and fifties, when women were supposed to smile and never make waves. I loved watching the events unfold as I got angry and broke one of society's and our family's basic rules. I often stood up to my father; sometimes it worked, and sometimes it didn't. As a teenager full of passion about what I believed in, I used to hang around the dining room table after dinner, sometimes for an hour, debating issues with my father. The issues could be anything from money to religion to women's roles in society. Mother would beg him (and some times me) to stop: "Oh, Bob, that is enough. Let's sit in the living room and watch TV."

But he would ignore her, and our debates would begin to turn into arguments, our voices getting louder. Eventually, she and my brother would leave the table. Many times my father said, "You should have been a lawyer, not a social worker." I don't know if that was a compliment or an insult; I heard it as the latter. In all my years of debating with my father, I don't ever remember him saying I was right. I think this is where I developed my need to be right.

JIMMY

Jimmy is one year old and doing what he loves to do: standing and leaning over with his head on the floor too. He is in front of one of our big Christmas trees with all the many presents and toys under it. This holiday was one of the most important to my parents, and Dad always picked out the biggest tree on the lot, put as many lights and ornaments on it as possible, and finished it off with the icicles, arranged perfectly, with the same amount of space between each one. We had to put them on one by one.

Jimmy is wearing his little yellow cotton shorts jumpsuit, which looks bright against his brown hair and big brown eyes. Every Christmas, my father set up the floodlights and took "staged" movies, which is how I remember much of my early childhood. Sometimes I ask myself, *What is real and what is movies?*

Then I am pushing a wheelbarrow with Jimmy sitting in it. I am wearing my favorite blue dress with the Polly Flinders smocking on the top. My blond hair is in long curls, and it is Christmas 1944, so I am four years old, and my brother is two. Jimmy's eyes are big wide circles of brown, and I am guessing he is scared.

Jim came to visit me in San Francisco in 1963. I have a picture of us on Fisherman's Wharf, looking at the freshly caught pink salmon laying on ice. I am wearing one of those net scarves to keep my hair in place. Jim smiles slightly, compared to my big laugh. He is so comfortable to be with. He doesn't talk a lot, compared to me, who talks all the time. We never get wild, and we don't party, but I enjoy his company.

When I was going through my tough times in the sixties, Jim came to be supportive. I was too fearful to make any major changes at that time. I have often wondered how my life would have been different if I had been able to accept his caring then. My kids would have had an uncle, and I would have had a brother.

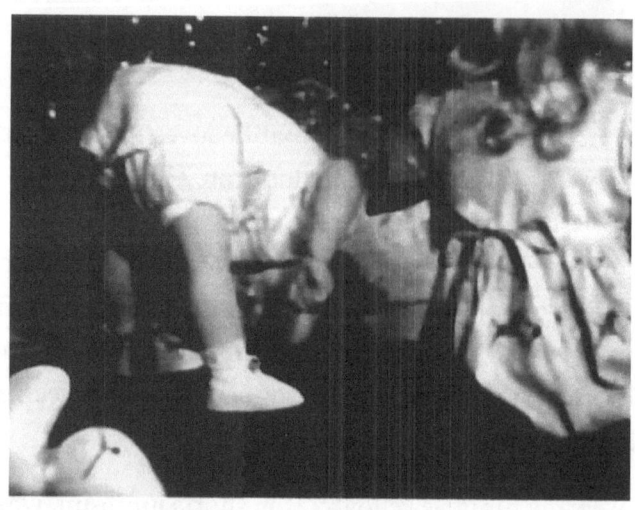

In August, 1966, Jim and Carol were married. Within a few years, they went through a difficult and painful time in their lives. I went to their home to be "helpful."

Unfortunately, I became inappropriately intoxicated, and hurt them both unbelievably. At that point, they chose to exclude me from their lives. This was forty-four years ago.

During the last couple of years, my lack of relationship with my brother has weighed heavily on my mind. A year ago, at the Good Friday service, I went down the aisle for the adoration of the cross, knelt down, and put my head down on that rough wood of the cross. I prayed a simple, short prayer: "Dear God, please intervene with my brother and me to heal our relationship. Please make me willing and give me the courage, should the time come, to apologize for my behavior that hurt him and Carol." That was it. I knew in my heart that God would answer that prayer. I just didn't know how or when.

It took me two days at the keyboard to write three sentences of apology to my brother. A week ago I saved it as a draft. I read it at least once a day, feeling the lump in my throat and the tears in my eyes. Two days ago, I brought the draft up again. I hollered over to our office manager, "Lauren! Should I send the letter to my brother?"

"Yes!" That was all she said.

I realized my finger was shaking, but I managed to push the SEND key.

It is over. I feel at peace. And God will take care of it. I let go.

EXTENDED FAMILY

Mildred and Mac McDowell were two of my parents' closest friends. We were "family," and Jane; her fiancé, Dean; and her brother, Jim, were always part of our holiday celebrations. I was a junior bridesmaid in Jane and Dean's wedding. Jane was beautiful, with her blond hair and blue eyes, and always my mentor. She was a dancer too, which was one of my fantasies. My mother said that Mildred McDowell always worked hard, both at home and at her job in the kitchen at St. Joseph's hospital. But she never complained. I still remember her chicken and rice, french-style green beans, and orange Jell-O with mandarin oranges. To this day, whenever I make this meal, I think of "Mid" McDowell. This picture was taken in the dining room at 1026 Downer Place. My mother loved flowered wallpaper, especially blue.

AUNT LOIS LITT AND COUSIN DAVE DUSELL

These pictures are from the home movies, Christmas 1945. Someone throws the panda to Aunt Lois. She catches it, rocks backward and forward, and seems to have such a good time. Dave is also laughing and enjoying himself. They seem to be having fun with my brother and me.

Aunt Lois married Uncle Larry Litt and moved to California when I was about fourteen. Those are about the only times we have any pictures of them and us.

My mother and her sisters are all attractive women. I don't know if they were close or not; my mother didn't talk much about her family.

MRS. KIPP'S NURSERY SCHOOL

"Time to go!" yelled my mother as she opened the front door of our 1026 Downer Place house. Mrs. Kipp, in her 1944 Dodge, drove up to the curb, threw open the door, and I jumped into the car. In those days, we obviously didn't worry about seat belts or any limitations as far as how many kids could squeeze into the car.

I was wearing my neatly pressed blue cotton dress, white anklets, and sturdy Buster Brown shoes. Mom had done my hair into two neat braids that day. And off we went.

The only memory I have of nursery school relates to our nap requirements. We had to take naps every day on our little mats. And apparently, I did not do this. So Mrs. Kipp took me aside, and I had to nap under her coat in a separate, dark room. What I most remember about this experience was the awful musty smell of her coat! There was no way anyone could go to sleep with that odor. So I faked it until I once again could sleep on my mat, with the other kids.

The little jungle gym was something I loved, and so my father bought one for our backyard. Eventually we had a full-sized swing and trapeze set, just like the parks. My dad's foundry, Love Brothers, Inc., was able to make those. Pretty exciting.

ANNUAL TRIPS TO ORLANDO, FLORIDA

"We really need to go to Florida since this may be Grandma's last year." I remember hearing my mother say that when I was five years old, and she said it every year until I was a sophomore in college, when Grandma died. She never said what was wrong with Grandma, but every Christmas we drove down to Florida and stayed in Aunt Sadie's half of this duplex. We spent one week with Grandma and Grandpa and the other week traveling the state, seeing such things as Cypress Gardens, Ringling Brothers winter quarters, the Everglades, Key West, Daytona Beach … A favorite activity was feeding the swans at Lake Eola with our neighbor Victor.

REVISITING GRANDMA'S HOUSE

In 2002, I visited my grandparents' home in Orlando. I was shocked to see the red front door. My grandparents would never have picked that color! I drove around the corner and saw where the orange and grapefruit juice manufacturing plant used to be. How many times we used to walk through the plant. The aroma of citrus juice was seductive.

Then I went to Lake Eola to look for the swans we used to feed. I found some swans, but they were all artificial. What a disappointment this was, as I had brought some bread to feed them.

I REMEMBER

I remember Sunday drives with my family. We drove out into the country and looked for farm animals. I remember my father getting out of the car and going over and mooing for the cows! How unlike most of my memories of my father, when he is prim and proper. After driving around, we then came home and had our fried chicken, biscuits, and gravy dinner. My dad and I were the "starch eaters," and we would compete to see how many biscuits with gravy we could eat. Then we would settle in to watch our favorite television shows: Gene Autry and his sidekick Pat Buttram; the Lone Ranger and Tonto; and maybe Roy Rogers and Dale Evans; Pat Brady and Nellybelle, his jeep; and Trigger, Roy's horse. Those were new programs in the 1940s and 1950s.

I DON'T REMEMBER

I don't remember what we did on Sundays after those TV shows. Did we stay home? I do remember eating Sunday night suppers that consisted of fried egg sandwiches with mustard on them. I think my dad used to cook them.

I DO REMEMBER

I remember sitting on the couch with the family. I remember my brother and I always getting "married," with me in a long yellow dress, and my parents sitting on the couch feigning interest in yet another "wedding." I don't remember anything more about Sunday nights. I do remember Saturday nights. Mrs. Miller would babysit when my parents went to bridge club or potluck group. She would make chicken pot pies. I would always watch *Saturday Night Hit Parade.* I thought Saturday nights were fun. The other thing I would do when my parents went out was go up into the attic and go through old things: pictures, mementoes, anything I could find. Even back then I was interested in getting to know my ancestors.

FIRST DAY OF SCHOOL

I wake up just as the sun is coming up, orange and gold streaking outside my window. My mother comes into my bedroom with her usual "rise and shine" routine, but today I am already awake, ready to jump out of bed. I have butterflies in my stomach in anticipation of my first day of school. My brand new red, green, and navy blue plaid dress and white bobby socks and brown oxfords are lying on the twin bed next to the one I awoke in. I run down the stairs to eat my Rice Krispies and skim milk before brushing my teeth and hair and heading out for school.

My mom gives me a kiss and hug as I head out the door. I skip part of the way, smiling as I go. I have already met my kindergarten teacher, Mrs. Smith. She has brown wavy hair, deep brown eyes that look like pools of chocolate, and a chubby body that feels so good when she hugs me and I melt into her. I am already imagining playing with the puzzles and games and listening to her read us stories. I start skipping again, anxious to get there.

Freeman Grade School, is my goal, which is twelve blocks away. I have practiced walking to school many times so I won't get lost. Our house, located at 1026 Downer Place, is actually in the Greenman Grade School district, but my parents pulled many strings to get me into Freeman because of the higher status of kids that attend there. I will find out later that my parents always drove, out of sight, in the car as I walked, just to make sure I knew the way.

I realize now that I have always loved "firsts": Monday, the first day of the week; the first day of the month; the first day of a new school year. I think this is because of all of the potential and possibilities that are present at the beginning of any event or project. I always start a new diet on the first, because my goal is to do it *perfectly*. Once I goof, I just let it go until the first day of the following week, month, or year. I only recently realized that I am still trying to *get it right* so that my parents will love me. I never knew how performance oriented my life was.

I feel sad for that little girl. She never knew how perfectly right she was doing things ... perfectly right for her.

DANCE LESSONS

I loved to dance and always wanted to be a professional dancer. This was as far as I got: I took ballet lessons at Miss Mulhern's Dance Studio in Aurora, Illinois, when I was five years old. Miss Mulhern weighed two hundred pounds, so she had an assistant who actually demonstrated the dance steps. Her studio was located on Stolp Avenue, on the second floor.

When it came time for the recital, I dreamed of wearing a tutu and pink leotards. They passed out the costumes, and I found out we would be ferns. My mother had a fit. And that was the end of my dance lessons.

I also took tap dancing for one year. The costumes weren't quite so bad, as you can see in the pictures. I don't know why I didn't take a second year.

When I was thirty-three, my dream came true, and I went to Fred Astaire Dance Studio in Downers Grove, took lessons, competed in contests, and even dated my dance teacher for a year. I loved it!

Two of the major issues that influenced my childhood value formation were gender and money. The following are reflections on these two subjects:

GENDER (1950–1960)

Sugar and spice and everything nice … This was the epitome of my mother's thinking, and it was how I was raised to be. I tried to look cute, and I always smiled—after all, as Aunt Sadie said, "Smile and the whole world smiles with you." I look at all of the pictures from these years, and I think I look sweet and naive, just like a girl should look..

Every once in a while, I remember thinking that *snakes, snails, and puppy dog tails* might be a bit more fun. But I learned to scream at spiders and all rodents, waiting for some strong, fearsome boy to rescue me.

I also learned not to be too smart, or if I was, not to let any of the boys find out. My mother said that "boys don't like smart girls." Even then, the innuendo was that the most important thing was to be popular, especially with the boys. Other childhood messages were that men are the breadwinners and women are the nurturers, who will obviously want to stay at home with the children. Women don't get angry, and women don't like sex (to like sex was considered promiscuous). Men love sex and have no control over their hormones, so it is up to the girls to remain chaste.

My mother also assured me that it was not feminine to be athletic, so I wasn't. The schools didn't encourage the girls to play sports, so I was in the majority.

There were times when I reversed the gender roles. One example was the electric train my father got for my brother. He mounted it on tracks on a large wooden support, and I just loved it. I spent hours playing with my dad with that train. I don't remember seeing my brother ever play with it.

When I started dating, I was told that girls *never* called boys and certainly never asked them to go on dates. I emulated my favorite fairy tale heroine, Cinderella. I worked hard, I waited for a fairy godmother to rescue me, and I hoped that Prince Charming would appear. A lot of my time was spent waiting and daydreaming, being passive.

I was sent to college at Northwestern University, which didn't fit at all with *don't be smart.* However, I met my husband, got engaged, and was married three days after graduation. At some level, I knew that the unspoken message was to also get my *Mrs.* So in 1962, I headed for San Diego to attempt to live out the "script" I had been given. Little did I know then, but after a full decade of attempting to do that, I would finally rebel, get divorced, go back to school for my MSW, and end up starting my own business.

MONEY MATTERS

"Have you checked your pockets, drawers, anywhere you might have put some change?" my dad asked each of us in the family. "As soon as you find all of your money, count it and give me the total, and please be exact."

It was January 1, any year, and my father was completing his annual New Year's Day ritual about money. Every year, he would add up all our money and keep track of it somewhere. I knew it was important to know how much our net worth was, but I wasn't sure why. When I was ten, my father taught me to keep a ledger, which I do to this day, and I find myself every January 1 listing all my assets and keeping track of my net worth. This apple hasn't fallen far from the tree.

The other interesting thing is that in spite of knowing how important money was, we never *talked* about it. I asked my mother one time how much money my father made, and she said, "Please don't ever ask your father that question." So, of course, I did, and he got angry and told me not to ask those kinds of questions. So in addition to money being important, it was also secretive, like so many aspects of my family history.

Growing up, I had ambivalence about money. I never thought we had a lot of money, but sometimes my friends would say sarcastic things like, "How would you know what it's like not to have money? You always have plenty!" And then I would find myself wondering how much was "plenty."

Money, along with sex, was one of those things nobody talked about. He was the president of Love Brothers, Inc., and often I worked in his office during summer vacations. The other girls would stop talking and whisper when I came around. They did not seem to want me in their "clique," perhaps because of his position.

It is only with hindsight that I realize we must have had money. Anyone who lived on Downer Place, west of Elmwood Drive, had money. But this never occurred to me while I was growing up. We lived in a two-story brick house with white columns on either side of the front porch. It was decorated in good taste but not extravagantly. We dressed conservatively too, in fashion but not showy.

When I was in high school, my father was given a family membership to the Aurora Country Club because of his job. I used to enjoy going there, and I had a group of six friends, boys and girls, one of whom I ended up dating in high school. My closest friends, however, swam at the public pool. My parents did not want me going there, although they never told me why. So I would ride my bike to the country club, ride over later to the public pool to meet my friends, and then pedal back to the country club to meet my parents for dinner. I never thought of that as unusual. To this day, I am equally comfortable with people who have more money and those who have less.

My father taught me that if you don't have the money, you don't spend it. That advice has helped me avoid any credit card debt in my adult life, and I am grateful to him for teaching me that. I remember it caused a conflict in my marriage when the water heater broke and we didn't have the money to pay cash for a new one.

"Just put it on the American Express," my husband said.

"No! If we don't have the money, we can't spend it!" I responded, true to my father's teachings.

"Well, I don't know about you, but I'm not taking cold showers! Now, put it on the American Express!"

And I did.

But that is the only thing—other than a house, a condo, and a car— that I have ever paid for over time. If I do charge something, I pay it off in thirty days.

Once I was with my mother in Peck & Peck's buying clothes for college. "Now, honey, let's get you some really *good* things so they will last a long time," she said. (I still have clothes that are twenty years old and totally out of style, but they have lasted well.)

"What about that pretty red suit?" I asked.

"Better to stick with basic black and navy blue," she replied. (I was forty before I started wearing red).

"Whatever you want," I agreed. (I always agreed).

My father also taught me to save for a rainy day. His philosophy was to save half of every raise. It would still seem like a raise because it was more money, but I would also build up my savings. I became a saver. But I also enjoy spending. I remember buying myself a mink coat for my fiftieth birthday. My husband and I were at the furriers, and the sales clerk kept talking to my husband. I was feeling irritated and said, "I would prefer if you speak with me. I am paying for this coat!" His eyes got big, his voice raised just a notch, and he said he was sorry. My husband looked at the floor, blushed slightly, and tried to ignore me.

I remember my father losing his job right after I graduated from high school in 1958. His new job took us to Milwaukee, Wisconsin. Four years later, he lost that job and took one in Oshkosh, Wisconsin. Since we never talked about money (or any problems, for that matter) no one told me this for several months. I was buying my wedding trousseau at the time, and I was extravagant with the lingerie expenditures. I remember feeling really guilty when I found out he wasn't working, and I offered to return the clothes. He wouldn't let me, and this made me feel even worse. I realize with hindsight that my father never allowed anyone to help him out.

One of my more painful memories is of my father complaining, "Do you have any idea how much you cost me? It was three thousand dollars for one year of college, for your braces, and for your wedding!" By then, it was too late to help with expenses or to cut costs, so I just felt bad.

I remember in high school, right after becoming a Christian at Young Life Camp, asking my father why he only gave one dollar a week to the church when he obviously made enough to be more generous. I do not remember his answer, but I do know he never gave any more.

When we met to settle my father's estate, Pat Cotter, his lawyer and friend, said, "I have never seen so much paperwork for this small of an estate." My father was compulsive in his recordkeeping. That was helpful to me, in starting my own business, although I had to learn to let go of the perfectionism.

A lot of my values around money have come from my father. Money, for money's sake, has never been very important. I like to be able to do things for the people I care about, perhaps take a trip or two, and occasionally stick my head into Chico's. But I am just as comfortable wearing clothes or shoes from Kmart. Although my daughter always says, "Just don't tell anyone, Mom!"

1950 CHRISTMAS CARD

The snow hung heavy on the trees behind us. The Chicago winds blew the snow around us in circular patterns as if we were in a snow globe. Here, I am ten years old, holding on to Jimmy, eight, and Duke, our cocker spaniel. I again remember how tall I was for my age, probably about five feet or taller. My brother comes just up to my shoulder. I felt embarrassed about my body; it seemed to grow and mature, completely out of my control. I shot up so fast, always the tallest girl in my gym class, first in line. And when they took our height and weight, one teacher shouted loudly to the other at the other end of the gym, "One hundred and fifteen pounds!" Then there were dance classes. The boys never reached my height, so they could never look me in the eye. They were usually looking at my neck or chest.

In addition to being "big for my age" (as the adults used to kindly say), or just "fat" (as the insensitive kids used to say), I had to wear those ugly leggings. "You'll freeze yourself to death," my mother used to nag in her attempt to be dramatic and make a point. She always won when it came to leggings. I also had to wear my brown orthopedic shoes.

And then there was Duke, who lived outdoors in a cage in the garage. My father had voiced his opinion clearly: "Dogs don't live indoors." No one questioned that authority. One of my most frightening memories is the image of my father sitting on top of Duke, beating him unmercifully, and hearing the yips coming from underneath him. Obedience was number one in my father's eyes.

I held on to my brother's hand, as I often did. Many times I felt responsible for and protective of him. He looked so innocent here, smiling without his two front teeth. It is probably good that neither of us knew what was in store for us in future years.

As usual, however, we are "lookin' good" on the Christmas card. "Keep up appearances" is what I learned from these experiences, and I learned it well.

MY BEST FRIEND

My best friend was Judy Brauer. She had brown hair that hung in long curls to her neck, soft brown eyes, and an inviting smile that made people want to come closer to her. In her one-piece pink play outfit at Mrs. Kipp's nursery school, she didn't stand out from the other little girls. But by the age of six, she did because she caught polio and was paralyzed from her neck down. She contracted polio the year before the Salk vaccine was discovered. I spent so much time with her that our parents and the doctors watched me closely, fearing I had caught it too. Her parents had a strong Christian faith. They always believed that what happened to Judy was God's will and divine plan, even when the nurse left the bed rails down and Judy fell out and broke both her legs. The next year, when the surgeon accidentally cut the only nerve that would have allowed her to walk, they accepted her permanent paralysis as God's will.

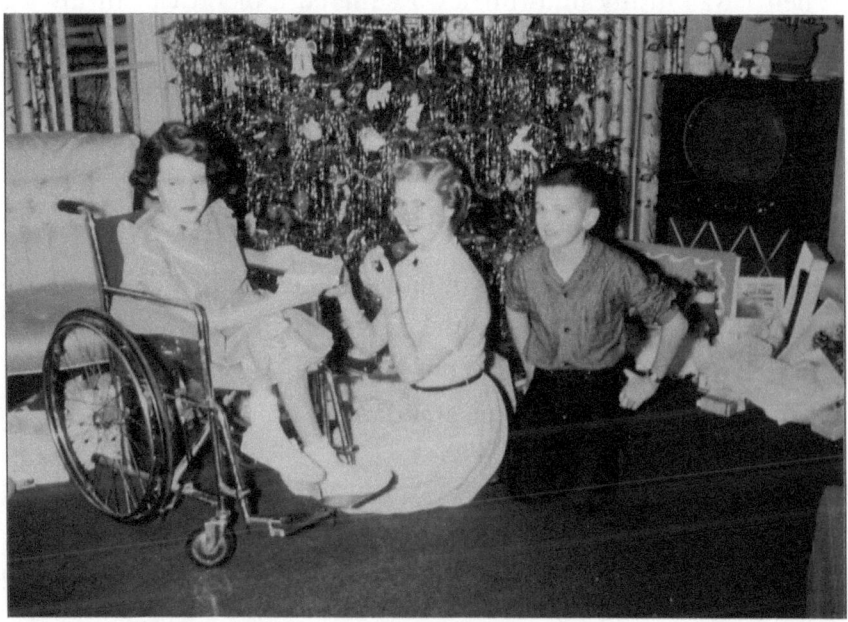

Judy reached more people from her wheelchair than most people do walking. I used to stay overnight almost every Friday. Her parents became my surrogate parents. In high school, Judy had all the Young Life meetings at her house, often fifty kids crammed into her living room, singing and listening to the leaders, Jan and Bill.

Judy was extremely bright and attended school via a walkie-talkie that had just been invented. It was fun to see who got to carry Judy to the next class. She got straight As, was editor of the yearbook, and never missed a dance.

Her father was an avid White Sox fan, and before long all the players on the team had heard of Judy Brauer. We used to have front-row box seats just down from home plate, toward first base. The players would stop and say hi. I was often included in these events. We stayed at the Palmer House, and I can remember pushing her wheelchair for long walks. One of the things I thought was most fun was running down the halls, just barely missing the people. How we both loved that!

When I was in my mid-thirties, I suffered a blood clot in my leg and was confined to bed for twelve weeks. Judy and I had daily phone conversations about God, our lives, and even death. I was not prepared, however, for her death. She talked to her father on the eve of her death and picked the songs and scriptures she wanted sung and read. The message was, "I am in a better place today."

One of my favorite pictures is of Judy and her family in 1964. She is holding my firstborn child, Scott. I drove him to Aurora to introduce him to Judy. How sad he could not know her longer, but this picture sits in my bedroom, and I look at it daily

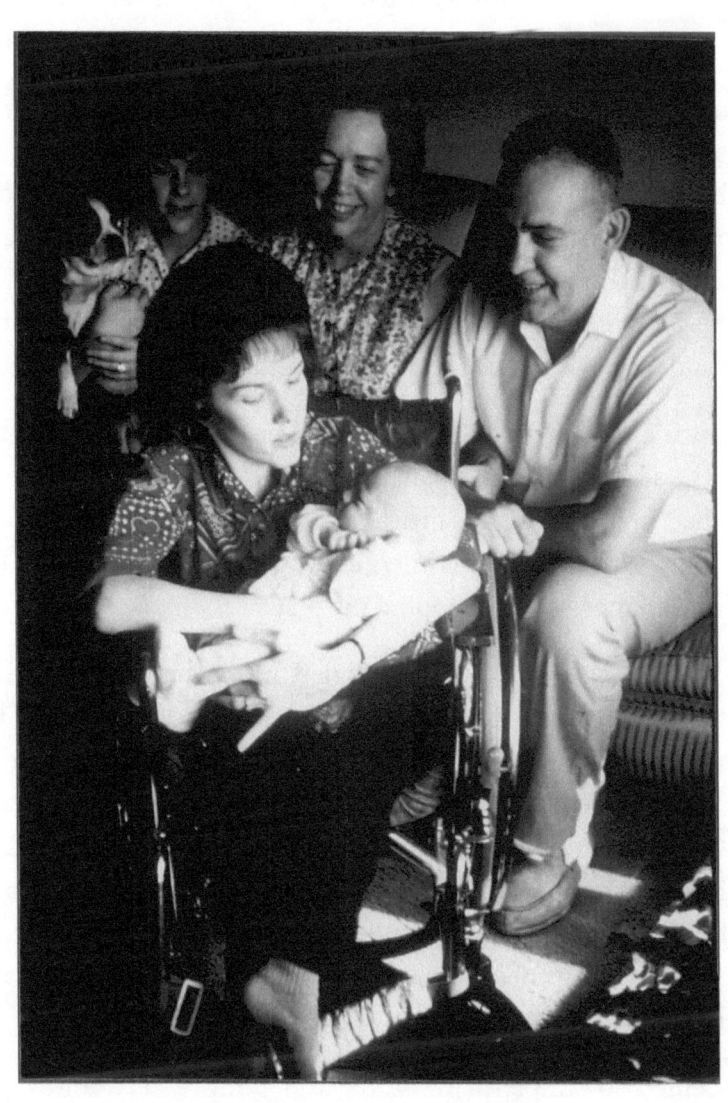

WEEKENDS ON THE FARM

Judy Myers was one of my closest friends in grade school. We used to play "horsie" at her house: run around on all fours and pretend we were horses. We also used to draw pictures of horses. But the ultimate fun was going to her farm in Sugar Grove for the weekend.

Judy has a pony named Pinto, and Pinto had a cart. Judy and I used to take Pinto and the cart out into the hay fields, where all we could see for miles was cut and baled hay. We would make up stories about meeting handsome men and riding off with them in the pony and cart, to get married and live happily ever after. We made a pact that we would name our daughters Debbie, and we both stuck to that.

There was a red barn as big as two of our houses, and we used to go up to the second level and play in the bales of hay. We used to play with the kittens up there—little black-and-white spotted ones, gray ones, and yellow ones. I was allergic to both hay and cats, but I don't have any memories of it stopping my play.

We also used to rescue the little piglets when they were first born, especially if one was a runt and the mother rejected it. We used baby doll bottles and took turns feeding the runts. We even named them, and they became our pets—little curly-tailed squealing pink babies. Eventually the animals were sold so we couldn't become too attached to them. I remember one of my worst memories on the farm was the slaughtering of a hog, hanging upside down, slit right through its middle, with insides exposed. I never went back again to view a slaughtering.

Life seemed so simple in those days. A pony, a cart, and a good imagination were all we needed to spend a wonderfully creative weekend.

SATURDAY BUS RIDES

The red and blue bus came to a halt. The door opened, and I stepped up into the bus. "Move it along!" shouted the bus driver. "All you girls going to the movies again?" I smiled, nodded, and moved to the back of the bus.

I was born and raised in Aurora, Illinois, on the west side. The one and only bus route intersected half a block from my house, at Elmwood Drive and Downer Place, the street where I lived. Running the entire length of Downer Place, from downtown to the west end of town, was a center parkway lined with tall elm trees, hence the name Elmwood Drive. The bus ran from downtown out to this corner. Then one route went as far as LeGrande Boulevard before it turned south and went around the loop and back to this intersection; and the other route went out to the far west end of town, turning south on Edgelawn, which in the fifties was the far west boundary of the town.

On some Saturdays, when I was in junior high school, a dozen of my girlfriends would get on the stop closest to their houses, and we would head downtown to the movies. On the short route, we would pass my house, a brick two-story home with two white columns on the front porch. A block west of that was the "Jones-Jones" house, a beautiful brick home, whose garage was said to contain an apartment worth forty thousand dollars! Around the corner was West Aurora High School, where many fond memories occurred.

If we took the long route, we would pass the "round house" on Edgelawn. It was a brick house, perfectly round. The mayor lived there. Rumor had it that he had a barber chair set up in his living room. I never ventured into his house, but sometimes we peeked in the windows and tried to see the barber chair. Three blocks south of that sprawled the Aurora Country Club. By the time the bus got back to Downer Place, on Elmwood, all twelve of the girls had piled onto the bus, and we would head east on Downer to downtown Aurora. This was a beautiful street, with the trees on either side touching their limbs and green leaves to form an arch under which the cars traveled.

We'd head down to the middle of town, crossing the bridge over the Fox River, past the Leland Hotel, where I spent many Saturday nights on the top floor, the Sky Club, dining with my family and dancing with many of my parents' friends. A block down from the hotel sits the Paramount Theatre, which still hosts many famous performers in the Chicagoland area. It has been remodeled in rich red velvet, with a huge stage and speaker system and an expansive balcony. Often we went to the Tivoli Theatre, which is no longer in existence. Many of the old stores such as Scensenbaugh's and Block & Kuhl's have been replaced by the gambling boat casino and restaurant, right across from the Paramount Theatre.

After the movies, we'd have french fries and milkshakes at the local restaurant, located on the bridge crossing the river. Then we'd catch our bus, head west, and each girl got off at her stop, while I rode the entire loop so I could spend more time talking with my girlfriends.

THE DRAKES

When I was in high school, my parents took us to California on the Amtrak Zephyr with the observation seating on top of the train. The Rocky Mountains and Feather River Canyon were some of the scenes along the way. My father got sick one night from the Apple pandowdy!

Here we are with my parents' good friends Jo and Evert Drake and their daughter Janet, taken in San Mateo, California. They used to live on Galena and LeGrande Boulevard, across the street from the high school. We went there after the East-West Thanksgiving Day football games.

The last time I saw Janet, she was driving around the country, visiting places from her lifetime and writing a journal about her experiences. Something like this.

LOST CHEERLEADING—JUNIOR YEAR

I am walking home from school. I have just lost the tryouts to become a varsity cheerleader my junior year. I am so disappointed, but I am terribly worried about my mother and how she will take it.

I hope she is not too upset, I think.

I wonder what I did wrong, I worry. *There* must *have been something else I could have done.*

What will my father say? I forget about Dad. He is always so interested in my being successful. Maybe he will be disappointed. Probably he will be mad.

I see my mother walking toward me. She calls out, "How did you do?" At only five feet two, she looks so small.

"I lost," I call back. My mother bursts into tears. Pretty soon they are uncontrollable sobs. I put my arms around her and hold her.

"It will be okay, Mom. I can try out again next year."

"But what will you do *this* year?" she gasps.

"Honest, I will be fine."

I am now aware of this reversal of roles. I comforted my mother when I was the one needing comforting. It had always been that way. No wonder I still have trouble comforting my inner child today!

DOWNSTATE IN '58!

After not being selected for cheerleading in my junior year, I made the squad in my senior year. I got to wear the blue Indian dress with the white fringe hanging under the arms, and the white moccasins on my feet. I was dating the basketball captain, and it was all like a dream come true. Reflecting back, I can see that in many ways it was my parents' dream, and I got there by following my parents' rules and values. "You must date someone in your own class," Dad was forever telling me. I still remember the time during my sophomore year when I was totally in love with Bob, who was a senior. I came flying in the door one day and shrieked, "Bob has invited me to the senior prom! Oh, please tell me I can go."

"You'll have to talk to your father," my mom told me.

That was bad news for me. My heart quivered, and I tried to figure out some way to convince him I had to go to the prom.

I brought the subject up at the dinner table. "Dad, all of my friends are going to the prom, and they want me to go, and Bob invited me to go. Oh, please—can I go?"

"No, you know the rules. Only same class dating," dad replied. "Otherwise, when you get to be a senior, you won't have any dates, and you don't want that, do you?" There was no emotion or feeling in his voice. I felt sick, partly because I knew there was no arguing with him when he made up his mind, and partly because the rule made no sense. So I had to deliver the bad news to my friends. I think my mother was on my side, but she would never stand up to my father.

Anyway, my parents succeeded. By my senior year, I was a cheerleader, heading downstate. So I guess it was worth it, at the time. I sometimes wonder what would have happened if I had ever been allowed to choose my own boyfriends, dates, and mates. Would my life have been different? Would I have been less apt to choose men like my father? Perhaps men like my mother? But at that point in time, I was happy. Or was it just "lookin' good" again? That was our family script.

They'll Make Champaign Rock

ournament time has found these West High varsity cheerleaders leading y, enthusiastic West Senior High student body in cheering the Blackhaw ctory through the regional, sectional and super-sectional tournaments. The ll set for Friday's opener against Springfield. Shown here, left to rig Jordan, Betty Ann O'Brien, Marlene Yount (captain), Pat Grover and Je (Photo by Spring Studio)

CHAPTER'S END

The young girl, carrying a crown of white flowers in her hands and accompanied by six other students, walked slowly around the West Aurora High School gymnasium. She looked into the eyes of several girls as the tension built to see who would be this year's prom queen. I glanced up to the balcony, and there was my mother. *Honestly, she looks more nervous than me!* I thought.

And then, after the four girls had been picked for the court, the young girl, attractive with short brown hair and brown sparkling eyes, stopped in front of me and smiled as she took my hand to lead me to the front of the gym. She put the crown on my head, and suddenly there was a rush of applause. And my mother's scream. I looked up again to the balcony, and my mother was leaning so far over the railing of the balcony that I wondered if she would fall. This was exciting for me, but I believe it was even more exciting for my mother. I realize now how she lived vicariously through me her entire life. This was the final climax of my high school years. She and Dad had worked so hard for this. I always had to date a boy in my class or I wouldn't have a date for prom. I had to try out for all the right things: cheerleading, a cappella choir, pep club, GAA, student council, National Honor Society, and on and on the list went. Always smile and always do what meets with others' approval. And so I was successful.

I graduated the following week and spent the summer preparing to go to Northwestern University, where I would be a small fish in a big pond, very different from high school, where I was a big fish in a small pond. I would "party hearty" and study little, which was also different from high school. Whereas when I left West Aurora High School, I was overprotected and had never drunk alcohol, smoked cigarettes, or used drugs, all that would change after the next four years, by the time I graduated from Northwestern.

We moved to Whitefish Bay, Wisconsin, that summer after high school, and I believe that this was a major transition point for our family. One of the reasons I chose Northwestern University was to stay close and connected to my Aurora friends. My mother's depression became significantly worse, as she had left all of her friends back in Aurora. Her alcohol consumption was now accompanied by the Valium her physician prescribed for her. I know now that the reason my father lost his job at Love Brothers in Aurora was his drinking, which was getting increasingly worse. I would sit in the kitchen and watch him pour a glass of vodka three-fourths full and top it off with 50/50, his favorite soda. "Please don't drink so much," I begged him.

"Don't worry about me," he would reply, and then he would pour a drink for my mother. Her drink would have about half the vodka and twice the 50/50 in it.

"But, Dad, the doctor said mom isn't supposed to drink!" I always reminded him of this.

"It's okay … as long as I keep an eye on how much she drinks," he said. Always the illusion of control.

And so our family moved into a darker time, in terms of my parents' alcoholism, the violence and abuse in the family, and the distance in our relationships.

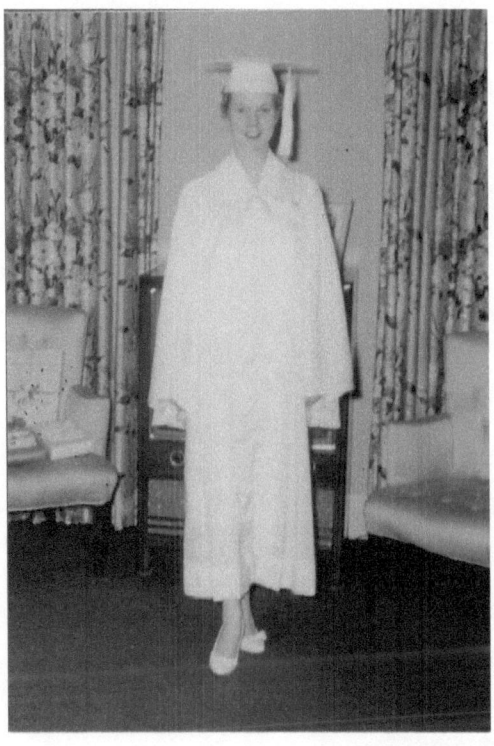

PATRICIA:
EIGHTEEN YEARS–PRESENT

BOOKS ARE A GIRL'S BEST FRIEND

Would you ever give away your best friend? Never in a million years! And at one, time my books were my best friends. I had several hundred at that point. I probably had six bookcases full of books, in categories such as women's books, spirituality books, psychology, substance abuse, and books on writing.

I loved to read, especially early in the morning. I think this represented my own personal time, when no one needed me and no one interrupted me. I kept getting up earlier and earlier so I wouldn't be interrupted by my family members (kids and husband). I currently live alone, but I still get up at four o'clock every morning so I can read and have my coffee for one hour. It is my favorite time of the day.

As a young girl, I loved to curl up on the green and yellow striped glider on my screened-in back porch, especially if it was raining and storming, and read. I had every book about Nancy Drew and the entire Cherry Ames series. I wanted to be a nurse at that time, and I just loved detective stories.

Part of my hanging on to the books, had to do with control, something I lacked in my alcoholic family system. I could always find a book if I needed it to look up some information for a paper I was writing. And God help the person who took a book without letting me know! It was as if some part of my life were missing. I actually felt a knot in my stomach at the thought of one of my books being unaccounted for. I think this was symbolic of my need to stay in control of my business when I had a dozen different offices. I am fairly laid back in my style of leadership. My staff pretty much decides when and where they want to work. So I am able to let go of a lot of control in those circumstances, but don't touch my books.

Another thing I realize is that books are a lot safer than dating. I won't get hurt by reading a good book, alone and with no demands on me. My relationship with a story is much more short term than it would be in a committed relationship with a mate, which might also explain my love of reading and the feeling of safety I get from my books.

I am extremely extroverted on the Meyers-Briggs test scores. If I want to energize, I spend time talking with others. But with reading books, I go *inside*. This is extremely nurturing for me, perhaps because it is one of the few times I spend that much time in silence and within myself. And it is an experience I cherish.

When I was in high school, I went to a Young Life camp in Colorado, fourteen thousand feet up in the air, near Mount Princeton. Every morning, I used to go out and sit on my rock, read my Bible, and watch the sun rise over the clouds. It looked liked a "silver lining" in my imagination. I always felt as if it were God telling me good morning. It was exhilarating.

One of my most valuable times is going up to Lake Geneva to my condo and spending the mornings watching the sun rise and reading a new book. I look out at the lake and find warmth in the beginning glow of the sun as it comes up over the horizon. I feel free from all responsibility except for myself. This feeling of freedom is like an eagle soaring in the sky. Up and up through the clouds, soaring in different directions, all by itself, in charge of its flight. How joyous it is.

About two years ago, I made a decision that I was going to stop hoarding my books and begin to share them with others. One of the reasons I hadn't done this was that I underline and take notes in the margins of my books, and I didn't look forward to having to do this project again if a book got lost. The second reason I was reluctant to share my books is that the notes in the margins said a great deal about me. By reading my notes, you could tell what my issues were, which ones were unfinished and why they still felt unresolved. And I wasn't sure I wanted to be that open with people.

I finally decided that I am who I am, and so what if other people don't like that? So I have started giving out many of my books for people to read. And I don't even keep any lists of who has which book. Such a sense of liberation I have experienced since I began doing this. My guts don't knot up anymore when I see a hole on the shelf, which means one of my books is missing. I figure that someone is enjoying it and will get it back to me when finished.

The lesson I am learning once again is this: people are more important than things. And I am also growing in my capacity for simplicity. I love the acronym KISS, which means "Keep it simple, stupid." Hopefully, I am doing just that. If the fact that I feel more peaceful and serene means anything, then I am succeeding.

MIDLIFE MANIA

What age did that speaker say midlife actually starts? I tried to remember. Certainly, at sixty-two, I must be somewhere in that category. How I had resisted that idea!

At the time, I was a successful psychotherapist with my own multisite business of twenty years. I had fifteen counselors and an office manager working for me. I had a passion for my work, especially with women and couples. Ever since I can remember, I have been a high-energy, up-early-and-work-long-days kind of person. Sick days were something I never considered. I have always been humbly grateful since I have considered my high energy and good health to be among my spiritual gifts from God. I believed that with all gifts comes a responsibility to use them in service to others. This had always been my life mission and purpose.

But suddenly, I felt as if my life was going to pieces.

Since the sale of my home went so smoothly, I trusted that this move was God's plan for my life and that God would guide my future decisions. I found an older town house, which I loved. Several people urged me not to buy it because of its age, but I felt drawn to it. This was to become my new home.

The sorting-through process was difficult. After packing twenty boxes of photo albums, scrapbooks, and family genealogy material, I experienced overwhelming sadness and grief. I wondered, *Will anyone want all these things? Will anyone carry on the traditions? Will anyone care?*

Getting ready to move forced me to address the major decision: whether to hang on to things or to let go. With each decision came a loss. I began to realize that this is the whole theme of midlife: holding on and letting go.

I valued being in control, yet everything felt out of control, including my body. I had always been slender and often wore a size four. But no matter what I tried to do differently, I was developing "love handles" and a tummy I could no longer hold in. If this was midlife, I would gladly give it to someone else, but I was not giving in to these changes! I saved one pair of size four jeans in the back of my closet, just in case.

I had been proud of my high energy level and how much I could accomplish in twenty-four hours. People consistently complimented me and were somewhat in awe of my achievements. My closest friends encouraged me to slow down, but I never had the time. I was too busy *doing* to take time for simply *being*. Besides, I had inherited a strong work ethic from my father, and I too valued being productive.

My faith and my church had always been a priority. Now I found myself filled with more questions and doubts than answers and faith. What was God doing to me? How would I figure out what Her spiritual gifts and goals were for the next part of this journey? There were days when I felt as if God had pulled away from me (or was it the other way around?), days when I felt a lingering lack of purpose and meaning.

Then the move. After selling and giving away so much of my stuff, I still could not fit half of it into my new town house. My garage was so full of boxes that I could hardly get my 2002 Chrysler pulled into the two-car garage. All the organization, the packing of essentials and bringing them over myself, was for naught. The movers simply piled boxes on top of the boxes I so desperately needed to get into, and they were too heavy too move.

I had two grown children at this point in my life: a daughter to whom I was close and a son who I rarely talked to or saw. This latter situation tugged at my heart. I had struggled with this for more than a decade, through the anger and hurt, followed by a sense of letting go, acceptance, and peace.

It was at this point that I had made the decision to downsize. I had remained in the large four-bedroom dream home that my former husband and I had built and lived in before our divorce one decade earlier.

This is too hard, I thought. *I'm tired of doing everything myself, of being so responsible. I want someone to take care of me for a change.* I started to cry, which was not like me at all. Maybe my life was going to pieces like Humpty Dumpty, and, like all the kings' men, I'd never get put back together again!

Since I couldn't even find my blankets, I pulled two beach towels from a shelf in the basement. I placed one on top of the mattress, crawled on top of it, and covered myself with the other one. I was so tired that I fell asleep in no time.

The next morning, I rose before the sun. As I sat quietly, reading my daily meditation book about grace and talking with God, I began to feel a sense of peace and serenity. The house had not changed—boxes all over, paint cans and tarp spread out in many of the rooms, everything in disarray—but something inside felt different. It was as if, by God's grace, I was able to let go: of my stuff, my weight, my faith, my children, and my former marriage. I could then surrender my life to God and live only in the present moment.

Is this the lesson I'm supposed to be learning? Is this what the midlife crisis is all about? When I live in the moment and focus inward, I feel the peace and serenity I have been searching for, regardless of external situations.

As I got dressed and began my first day in my new home, I looked up and said out loud, "Okay God, you're in charge. Once again, I surrender my life to you and your will. So far, you've done a pretty good job; we'll do the next leg of this journey together too."

Suddenly the issue of age and midlife did not matter at all. What mattered for me was *how* I lived my life, not *how old* I was. To me, this transformation was another example of resilience and the ability to change.

MOTHER EARTH

For twenty-five years, Gale and I have shared a monthly meal. Her engaging smile and deep blue eyes say, "I'm interested in you." When she gives me a hug, I feel as if the earth wraps itself around me like a thick, warm quilt. I call her "Mother Earth." She is part of my family of choice.

In her early sixties, Gale is small-boned, of a medium height, and has an olive complexion and naturally wavy brown hair. She calls herself the "Jewish princess," and a bit of her New York accent still lingers.

Gale is an empathic, focused listener, nonjudgmental and supportive. She leans forward as I speak and looks at me so intently that I feel I am the only person in the world, that nothing and no one else matters

The crow's feet wrinkle around her eyes when she laughs her guttural, raspy laugh. She appears to also be chuckling about some inner private joke.

Gale is intelligent, articulate, and freely speaks her opinions. She is assertive and asks for what she wants. Some would call her an "uppity" woman. A loyal friend, she keeps her commitments and has relationships that span decades.

Profoundly in tune with the earth's cycles, Gale often attends special celebrations of the solstices. She feels deeply connected, both with the women there and with nature.

She is unpretentious, solid, and grounded. Her dress is comfortable yet stylish. Crinkly cotton skirts and loose-fitting blouses give her a feminine and flowing appearance. Earth tones are accented with turquoise and orange and large Native American jewelry. She is slow and graceful, unhurried and calm.

Creativity and risk taking are a part of this wise woman. She often travels by herself for weeklong creativity conferences. Her trips, from New Mexico to Canada, result in exquisite photos. From New Mexico, she once gave me a picture of a small clay Indian house with a big cross on the front. Her eyes sparkled when she said, "There was *no cross* on the house when I took the picture! I knew you would love it." And I did.

Her creativity and patience are exemplified in the storybook she made for her granddaughter, the newest "princess." Each page is handwritten with a special snapshot of the two of them, covered with Saran Wrap so it won't get soiled. Such a gift!

Gale is a psychotherapist who works with rape victims and motherless daughters. She also teaches in the Women's Studies Program at the local college. Her favorite form of therapy is couples therapy. A long-time feminist, she believes in the equality of all human beings. She is an empowered women who is comfortable with herself. Best of all, she can laugh at her own human foibles. I count among my greatest blessings the friendship of this wise and caring "Mother Earth."

FRED ASTAIRE DANCE LESSONS

Ever since I was a little girl, I always dreamed of being either a dancer or an ice skater, like Sonia Henie. At age thirty-seven, my dream came true. When I saw the ad in the newspaper—"Are you single? Do you love to dance?"—I talked a friend of mine into going to check it out with me. By the time I walked out the first night, I had spent several thousand dollars on future lessons. I never spent money like this, and since I couldn't get out of the contract, I decided to make the best of it. I had two of the best years of my life: two lessons each week and a free Friday night dance party. I loved it! I competed in several dance contests in Chicago and won some awards. My costume consisted of a ten-dollar handkerchief dress from Sears and a hundred dollars worth of black ostrich feathers from New York, sewn to the bottom of the dress. As long as I could follow my teacher's lead, it was a cinch! I was never happier than when I was dancing. It was like a dream come true.

BETRAYED BY MY BEST FRIEND

"How could you have done this to me? You've been my best friend for four decades—most of my life!" My question was not addressed to a person but to the long white cigarette.

I closed my eyes. *How could* you *have done this?* I asked myself. *You— the addictions counselor; you—who keeps rationalizing your nicotine addiction because you only smoke the lowest tar cigarettes?*

This all began one Monday, August 19, 2002, with my annual routine chest X-ray (normal X-rays had allowed me to rationalize forty-two years of smoking). By the next afternoon, I was reading written test results that described a five-by-ten centimeter mass in the lining of my left lung. My heart was racing, my throat was tight, and my mind told me I had six months to live … and the first thing I did was reach for my best friend—a cigarette.

I still remember my first cigarette, spring of 1960, my sophomore year in college. I sat on the edge of the bed, legs crossed yoga-style. I inhaled deeply, feeling light-headed as I learned how to smoke. I had decided to take up black coffee and cigarettes in order to lose the twenty pounds I'd gained during freshman year. And it worked. The ugly pounds dropped off. For the next forty-two, years I maintained my weight of 115 pounds with black coffee and cigarettes.

It occasionally crossed my mind that God might not condone my smoking, but I got validation from all sorts of places. Even Jane Fonda and Mother Superior in the movie *Agnes of God* claimed that "if Jesus were here today he'd probably smoke!"

That night, I knelt down by my bed and prayed: "God, I know you don't make deals. I pretty much believe you can heal me if you want to. How about if you remove my mass, I'll quit smoking?"

I had a repeat chest X-ray and a CT scan three days later and then took off to Lake Geneva, Wisconsin, to spend the weekend in my getaway condo. I smoked, drank coffee, read, and wrote all weekend. I decided that if I had to quit smoking, I would *never* again have a creative thought or be able to write. I wondered if that was how Hemingway felt about his alcohol.

Eight days after the initial X-ray, I got the phone call from the nurse. She said, "The mass is gone, and the doctor wants to see you tomorrow."

At the appointment, the doctor said, "There is no tumor. The mass was a shadow from the skin folds on your back. Your lungs are completely healthy."

My first words: "Maybe I don't have to quit smoking."

She said, "Wrong."

The doctor was a forty-year-old female with wavy black hair and some freckles, who bounced around her office and laughed a lot. *Probably never even touched a cigarette,* I thought bitterly. *What does she know?* She asked if I had any symptoms. I said no. But I didn't tell her about the wheezing in my lungs; the fact that my voice had lowered two octaves and sounded hoarse much of the time; and the repetitive, shallow cough.

Since I was heavy as a child and gained all that weight in college, I was petrified of gaining weight. I plopped my leg up on the doctor's desk, grabbed two inches of fat on my thigh and stated emphatically: "This is fat, *not* muscle, fat. If I quit smoking, I will become obese!"

The doctor kept writing on her chart. At one point, I wondered if she was writing about my mental health.

On the way back to my office, I listened to a stop smoking hypnotherapy tape, which I did every time I was in the car. The man's voice was low, singsongy, soft, and slow. He talked about how wonderful healthy pink lungs are, and I thought, *So what? I just want a cigarette.* He said, "You're feeling better than you ever have in your life." I thought, *The hell I am! I'd just love a cigarette.*

I chose not to tell my daughter, now thirty-five years old and a psychotherapist like myself, because I was afraid she'd say "I told you so." I finally did tell her, and she said, "I love you; I want you to be around for a long time to watch your grandsons grow up. Besides, you *have* to quit—you promised God." Which brought me full circle to where I began.

I was scared. On September 1, 2002, I gave up a forty-two-year-old addiction. Recently, I have thought of a new definition for Christian/ spiritual growth: Giving up one addiction after another until there's nothing left to cling to except God.

An exercise a friend gave me, based on Ecclesiastes 3:11, suggests making two lists: (1) things God might be calling me to do; and (2) things I need to relinquish to respond to this call. Are there any signs this has already begun? Oh, yes, I haven't had a cigarette today!

Betrayed by my best friend? An error by the X-ray technician who allowed skin folds? Or an intervention by a loving God who has other plans for me? I choose to believe the latter.

A sense of place is important to my life story. The following pieces address this issue.

MY NEIGHBORHOOD

I have always loved Tudor homes, so when I downsized from my big house in 2002, it was natural to want to look at these town houses. My Realtor wanted me to pick anything but these. He thought they were too old and showed me larger, more expensive places to live. But when we walked into this house, my daughter took one look at its bright, cheerful, inviting interior and said, "Oh, Mom, this is so you!" And she was right. In back of the house, a brick patio with a bubbling pond to one side backs up to a forest. Even though the forest is only one city block, in the summer, with the dense foliage and its many shades of green, it appears to go on forever.

In the morning, as I drive to work at 7:00 AM, I see at least two dozen people walking their dogs: large brown and black Labs, miniature white poodles, and everything in between. The neighbors are all retired, laughing, talking, and appearing to enjoy socializing with each other. I have often thought of buying a dog for this reason.

My street is a hefty hill, especially if I am out biking and am on the return trip. Mostly people are walking, and they offer friendly, welcoming waves, as I ride by.

The houses look exactly alike. Even the windows with the white crossed wooden bars in them are just like the rest. Every once in a while, there is a bright blue open umbrella on somebody's deck, which catches my eye. But otherwise, all the same. Rather than being boring, it adds to the sense of tranquility.

In June, there is a garden walk, and for good reason. Everyone who lives in the area seems to have completed Gardening 101. My neighbor's entire front yard, which we share because I don't have one, is her garden. She has at least one hundred multisized rocks in her rock garden. There is a "bottle tree," an evergreen with its branches cut short and needles pulled off. Various colors and shapes of bottles have been pushed onto the ends of the branches. They do this in Georgia, her former home. The hanging planters are gorgeous: striped, red, blue, yellow, every color of the rainbow. She has an old wicker rocking chair outside her front door so she can sit and enjoy the outdoors: yellow sunflowers, red roses, smaller cabbage plants, multicolored pansies. I sit in my living room each morning, eat my breakfast, and enjoy her garden.

The air smells fresh. It is quiet and peaceful. I love sitting at my kitchen island, sipping my morning cup of coffee and looking at the forest, reading my book, watching the sunrise, and listening to the silence. The tranquility of this place is magnificent.

DOWNSIZING: MY NEW HOUSE

"This place is *so you!*" my daughter exclaimed.

"I really do like it a lot, even though my Realtor definitely does *not* want me to buy this place," I responded. I felt a warm attraction to the town house.

I remember just like it was yesterday. On the one-year anniversary of 9/11, my neighbor was having a neighborhood coffee in honor of the date. Midway through, I made the decision and announced I was selling my house. I had planned on doing this for the last ten years, since my divorce in 1992. My four-bedroom house was gorgeous, but I needed only a couple of the rooms to live in. That afternoon, my neighbor and her husband walked over, made an offer, and my big house was sold. It must be time to downsize.

My Realtor, a personal friend, showed me some big beautiful and expensive town houses. Finally, I asked him if there were any homes for sale in Wheaton Oaks. He said there was only one and it was very old, with the original owners and decorating. I insisted on seeing it. I took my daughter and her family, in from California, to see it too. My daughter's husband, a builder, said the kitchen floor was uneven—not a good sign. Old-fashioned half walls divided the living and dining rooms and the kitchen and small office.

I fell in love with the tall vaulted ceiling over the fireplace in the living room. I decided to buy the place. I brought my decorator over, who walked through and took extensive notes, and I was off on a new adventure.

I moved in January 2003, on the coldest day of the year. The mover said, "You'll never get that grand piano in there. And the huge television console won't go down into the basement family room." They both fit.

Becky, my decorator, thinks "big." All the lighting fixtures came down and were replaced with modern ones. The pictures and wall decorations came down. A decorator mirror that went all the way up into the vaulted ceiling graced the living room wall.

The first thing Becky did was paint the entire downstairs a light green. I am not a lover of green, but it is stunning. I mentioned I would miss the kitchen island from my old house, and she responded, "Tear out the half wall and put in an island." And so it went.

The kitchen is on the back of the town house, and it looks out onto a brick patio, a small pond, and what appears to be a forest of trees. Actually, it is only a city block, which is apparent in winter, but in summer, when the foliage is in full bloom, it looks like it goes on forever. And if I open my bedroom window directly above, I hear the birds singing and the pond gurgling.

My treadmill is on one side of the basement, so I walk every other day. A small TV with DVD player allows me to watch movies while I walk.

This downsizing was a major turning point in my life. It forced me to get rid of a lot of "stuff" and to simplify my life. I invited friends over in May 2003 for a house blessing, led by our pastor. We rang bells in each room, read scripture, and then shared refreshments and time together. Ever since I moved into this community, I have felt safe, secure, and serene.

MY SAFE PLACE

I look out my kitchen window on the back of my town house, and I see the full moon. I love the full moon, full of hope and magic. The stark bare branches of the oak tree in my back yard crisscross in front of the moon, making an interesting pattern. I could stare at the moon forever. There's something about the moon that makes me think of a goddess. Perhaps because its monthly cycle seems feminine.

It's around ten degrees outside, minus sixteen degrees with the wind chill. I also know there are twelve inches of snow on top of my round metal table on the patio and on the light-colored round concrete bird bath with the two concrete birds, one on each side of the bath.

I can't see anything except for the moon and the bare branches because it is still dark. I enjoy getting up while it's still dark, pouring myself a cup of coffee, and settling in to read my book on how to write a memoir. I feel excited by the experience of anticipating the rising of the sun and the turning from dark into light. This experience is like my life, going from dark to light, from ignorance and denial to enlightenment and insight—and the excitement that goes with it.

I'm sitting in my tall swivel oak chair at the kitchen island. My kitchen cupboards are white, and the granite counter tops are light. My curtains have red and green accents, which brightens up the room. My countertop and oak hutch contain pictures of my grandchildren and me. Each time I visit the boys in California, I insist that the first thing we do is to take a new picture for Nanee's office and her kitchen. They're not thrilled with this, but they tolerate it because they know how much it means to me. My solid-looking oak hutch is about eight feet tall, the top part enclosed with decorated glass panes. It matches the round oak table placed directly in front of the windows. The green credenza, painted with pretty white and yellow flowers, has two drawers that hold my table linens. There is a small decorative lamp with metal pink flowers and green leaves winding up the black metal stem. It matches two picture frames that I have on the hutch, with the metal pink flowers and green leaves. Several of the picture frames have lavender and yellow pansies on them, my favorite flower. I also have a wreath of pansies hanging over the door. I love the feeling of the kids being so close to me—at least they are close in my heart.

My town house represents freedom and independence for me. When I come home at night and close and lock the front door, I know that I am exactly in the right place for me, a place that I chose for myself, even against my Realtor's opinion, and which I have absolutely no regrets about choosing. I intend to spend the rest of my life in this home.

MY CONDO

It is still dark, but the birds begin to chirp. I look out over the porch of my condo and see the graceful weeping willow tree with its low branches that droop almost to the ground. To the other side of the porch is the Asian tree with the reddish buds, expensive and beautiful. To the left of the weeping willow, I see the swimming pool with the deep blue-green water and the white chairs, umbrellas, and tables lined up around it.

The sky is beginning to brighten, a hint of sunlight to the east. Shades of red, orange, and yellow begin to light up the horizon. I love the large weeping willows. I, like them, try to be flexible and adaptable, as opposed to rigid and controlling. They grow fast and large, and their branches are wispy in the gentle breeze as they dance slowly from side to side. What an example of being resilient!

I can hear the silence. It calms and soothes me. No sounds other than the birds. In a few hours, I will hear people talking and laughing, children swimming in the pool, motorboats not far from my condo on Lake Geneva. And it won't end until dark. So I cherish this quiet time of sunrise. It rained last night, and a layer of dew on the grass shines and glistens. I am reading and devoting all my attention to my book. No phones to answer, no one needs me, no one talking … just silence and the rising of the sun. The sky is getting brighter now, and I see the sun coming up. I feel a sense of sadness that this time of silent waiting and anticipation is over. But it is also a new day, a new beginning, and although at one time in my life I feared new beginnings, I now look forward to them.

THIRD PLACE

It used to be that people hung out and socialized in bars, grills, and coffee shops, but in the baby boomer generation, with its focus on health, wellness, and prevention, one of the major hangouts today is the health club. This is a place for all ages—they have a nursery for young moms and specials for middle-agers—but the largest group of members I see "hanging out" is the seniors, those of us over sixty-five who are retired (or supposed to be retired)! We go there to stay fit and also to hang around after our workouts and just drink coffee and socialize.

By 9:00 AM, there are no parking places left, and I find myself getting irritated, driving around looking for someone who might be leaving. Three cars hover, with their blinkers on, waiting for that one place. Not exactly a friendly group at that point.

Upon entering the health club, three smiling faces wait to swipe my membership card. I think, *No problem for them: twenty-something and thin; I would be smiling too.* But I return the smiles, hand over my card, and head off for the locker room. I can hear the hum of the hair dryers. Some of these women are fortunate enough to know how to redo their hair each day. Not me. My hairdresser has total job security, knowing that she is the only one who knows how to fix my hair in such a way that I am presentable for my professional life. I smell the hair spray, lotions, and perfumes that the women use to transition back to their non-workout lives.

Upstairs, as far as my eyes can see, are people on the elliptical, StairMasters, treadmills, and bicycles. It looks like a robot colony, with the individuals doing their own activities: walking, climbing, riding, staring blankly at the small television screens in front of them, or wearing tiny white plugs in their ears, connected to wires that attach to the small adapters on the handlebars of their machines. Lost in another world, none of the people even seem aware of who is around them, much less acknowledge their neighbors on the machines next to them. This is how they will spend the next forty-five minutes. And they do this three times each week.

Other people are lifting weights, sitting on machines that give resistance to the movement of their arms or legs. They look miserable: frowning, grunting, and groaning. If someone came to visit from another planet, he would certainly question our idea of entertainment, until we explained how good this is for us: "No pain, no gain!"

After their entire bodies are crying out to stop, some people get dressed, pour cups of coffee, and hang out in the chat area. For many, this is their major social group, and being with them is equally as important as working out. I can hear low talking, probably the latest gossip, and lots of laughter among the folks. They look like they are having a good time, especially now that they are out of the grasps of the machines.

Here are some more of my "family of choice": Penny and John, Mary and Ev, Gale and Beth.

FUN FRIENDS

"Let John go get the camera!" Penny shouted. "Just leave your dark glasses on; you look just like a movie star." I never knew quite what to expect when I dropped off their Christmas present, and this year was no exception. John showed up with his camera *and* with his Santa Claus hat.

But there is a serious, kind, and caring side to both of these folks. Friends for over a quarter of a century, we have seen each other through many of the more difficult times in our lives. I can always trust that these folks will be there when I need anything.

There is the annual trip to my condo to meet with the wasp exterminators and to make sure they inspect every inch inside and out so I feel safe going up there during the summer.

And there was the year they decided I needed a pre-lit Christmas tree (I was still putting my tree together limb by limb, and then putting on the strings of lights), and so they went and got one for me and came over and put it up.

I am so grateful for good friends like this.

MARY AND EV

My two dear friends Mary and Ev helped me celebrate my birthday a couple of years ago. Mary and I have hung out together for over three decades, and Ev joined the picture over two decades ago.

Mary is such a kind soul, and she reaches out so often. She is an RN, and so she was my first line of defense when I eventually got lung cancer and swine flu. She simply took charge, and I could relax and take care of myself as I needed to.

When I think of Mary, I think of gardens. Her garden takes up most of her backyard and is beautiful! We often sit on her swing and talk, looking at the flowers and bird feeders and the goddess statue that is a fountain.

Ev is always there too. So many times he has come over to help me put Christmas decorations back into the crawl space because I am so claustrophobic. He is a handyman and knows how lots of things work.

Mary's son, Kurt, is like another son to me. I was shocked a few years ago when the Harley riders came by in the Fourth of July parade, and I heard him shout, "Hey! Mrs. Pape!" I flew out and gave him a big hug.

THREE FRIENDS

Over thirty years ago, when Beth worked as the coordinator of Information and Referral Services for DuPage County, Gale was in private practice and working at the YWCA, and I was working for the Diversionary Division of the DuPage County Probation Department, the three of us began getting together for some kind of meal on a monthly basis. We were three social workers trying to make the world a better place, and when we got together, we would share our personal lives related to our families, goals, and dreams.

We kept track of our relationships, or lack thereof. Beth and Chris got married down by the Riverwalk in Naperville. We spent a weekend in Lake Geneva, where Chris showed us how fast he could drive the boat. We always got together for Christmas and exchanged gifts. We watched each other grow, change, and become wiser.

One thing that never lacked when we got together was laughter—at each other, at ourselves, and at the little ironies of life. As long as we could learn from our experiences, then nothing was lost.

We kept track of kids and grandkids, and we grew older together. There is nothing better than three friends … especially three *social worker* friends.

SWINE FLU

In thirty years of being in business, I had never taken a sick day. In fact, my office manager said she has been here for four years and has never even seen me sick. Well, last week took care of that: I took a "sick week."

For four hours Thursday night (November 19, 2009), I felt as if people were taking knives to my entire body and stabbing me as hard as they could. I don't remember ever having such pain. And then I had such bad chills that I couldn't hold still. It felt as if someone had beat me up and left me on the road. My doctor said that was the number one symptom of the flu. He also said that there was really no test for the H1N1 virus, so if someone showed up in his office with flu symptoms, he just assumed it was H1N1 because he wasn't seeing the other strains in DuPage County. Although he said it was just a name, I was sitting there thinking that I didn't plan on telling anyone what I had. I think I might have some understanding of how the lepers used to feel. I pictured telling someone sitting next to me at church, and suddenly I saw the pew empty out.

I came into work last Friday but ended up lying on the couch until we could get to the urgent care facility, where it turned out I had a temperature of 104! They took me home, with antibiotics for the infection and Tylenol for the fever. I didn't even think I owned a thermometer.

My friend Mary, an RN, came over twice a day to feed me some ginger ale and chicken noodle soup. I was so exhausted, I could only sit with my head lying on the kitchen island countertop. I was sleeping twenty-three hours out of every twenty-four. I had no interest in anything at all, a frightening way to live since I generally have a great deal of passion about everything.

By Tuesday, my fever was gone, but I wasn't allowed to go to work until it was gone for two days. So I asked a friend to take me to the Jewel delicatessen, where I picked up chicken salad and macaroni salad—and that was my Thanksgiving dinner. I was really thankful, however, to have my health back again, and hopefully I will never take it for granted. Another example of resilience? Perhaps.

FIFTY-YEAR OLD CHRISTMAS RITUAL LAID TO REST

"Just try them. You'll like them," my father said in his most convincing voice. I was resisting trying anything new. The shrimp and scallops on the Fish Platter looked anything but inviting. Eventually, he won out, and at ten years of age, I became an avid lover of shrimp—cooked, cold in a shrimp cocktail, little shrimp in shrimp salad ...

For the last fifty years, we have had a Christmas ritual my mother started when I was a child. Every year, she would cook tons of shrimp, chill them, make a hot cocktail sauce, and put them all on a tray with Ritz crackers. This was our afternoon entertainment every Christmas Day. That is, until May 2007, when I had a follow-up CAT scan for my lung cancer surgery. About six hours later, I developed a rash all over my midsection and the doctor said it was an allergy to iodine. This could not be. Because if I was allergic to iodine, then I would be allergic to shellfish!

I went to an allergist, and he tested me negative for being allergic to shrimp. So in 2007, I did my all-afternoon shrimp fest. And all was well. I never thought about it again.

Then I did the same thing in 2008. Within a day or two, I developed hives under the skin on my cheeks. Oops. Theresa, our "in-house nurse," said I had better get it checked out at urgent care since I was flying to California the next day for Christmas. Sure enough, they put me on steroids and Benedryl.

So this year, back I went to get tested again for an allergy to shrimp (I sure am reluctant to give this up, aren't I?). And this time the doctor asked me a different question: "Just how many shrimp do you eat? More like two or three ... or more like two dozen?"

"Uh, more like two dozen," I admitted. So they repeated the test, which again came out negative. But this time the phone call from the nurse recommended eating two or three shrimp. My first thought was, *That's not even worth it!* Spoken like a true addict!

Then something Lauren said yesterday got my attention. She said, "How much do you *really* like shrimp? Is it really worth all this?"

And of course the logical answer was no!

So tomorrow I will cook the last bag of raw shrimp (I have two bags of forty shrimp in my freezer!). And I will allow myself to have three shrimp before I put this ritual to rest. All I can say is that the older I get, the harder it is to keep letting go of the things I think I can't let go of!

CHILDREN

FIRST PREGNANCY AND CHILDBIRTH

My husband and I lived in an apartment at 3900 Iowa Street in San Diego, California. I went home to Wisconsin to visit my parents. While I was home, Dr. Pansch told me that because I had a tipped uterus, I would have trouble getting pregnant. So we began trying as soon as I got home, in September 1963. Nine months later, the same doctor delivered my first child!

I felt wonderful during my pregnancy. I ate healthy: lots of cottage cheese, tomatoes, veggies, and fruits. I walked a mile every day. And I always got eight hours of sleep at night. I have often laughed and said, "If I just had the temperament for lots of kids, I would have done that—because I never felt better or healthier than when I was pregnant."

San Diego, California

My best friend and neighbor, Sara Aasland, joined me with Velma
Aishman, the apartment complex manager, in learning how to sew.
I managed to sew all my maternity clothes. This was a good place to
start because they didn't have to fit. Mostly they were full circles that
simply expanded to fit me as I grew. I loved the blue-flowered cotton
dress the best. I really hated sewing the pants because I couldn't get
the stretch panels in right. I remember one time I went out and the
stretch panel was so big that the pants kept falling down. I ended up
using part of a clothesline to hold them up. Mrs. Aishman had a fit
about that.

I had started working for the San Diego Welfare Department in
September 1963. Fortunately, I didn't show for quite awhile. I do
remember my supervisor asking me a couple of times if anything was
wrong, that I looked "pale." And then came the day when I was six
months pregnant, still wearing a regular dress with a full skirt that
was tight around the waistband, and I fainted. By that time, I had to
admit to my supervisor that I was pregnant. They had a rule that no

one could be more than six months pregnant and still work for them, so I had to quit.

Mother's Day
Honolulu, Hawaii

In May, I asked my doctor in California if I could fly over to Hawaii for Mother's Day and join my husband at Fort Derussey on the island of Oahu. Graz, his grandmother, had offered to go with me. My doctor said that the worst thing that could happen was I'd have the baby in Hawaii. So he wrote me a permission letter for the airlines. I flew over and stayed for three weeks. I have pictures of us at a Hawaiian luau. I even got up on the stage and did the hula dance! On Mother's Day, I received a Hawaiian lei made up of fresh white and purple flowers. We toured the whole island, and the only time I had any problem was on the *USS Arizona,* when I got seasick. I flew back after three weeks. I felt great, but I remember that the stewardesses were really worried about me. I went home to my parents' home in Oshkosh, Wisconsin, to await the birth.

I lived in my blue and white pregnancy bathing suit. It was hot, and I was uncomfortable. I had gone home to my parents' home specifically because they convinced I wouldn't know what to do if I was alone in California, and this way they could help me out. So when my water broke on a Saturday morning, I went and told my mother. She got hysterical, started rushing around the house shouting instructions, and in general added to my already anxious state.

So I did what any perspective mother would do: I went into the bathroom, washed my hair, and started the one-hour process of putting my hair up into a French twist so I would look nice for the delivery. My pains were about a half hour apart and we had a one-hour drive to the hospital. By midmorning, my mother had called the doctor at least six times. He said to come to Theda Clark Hospital in Neenah-Menasha.

When I got to the hospital, there was no doctor because he could not believe that my labor was going that fast with my first child. I was alone because my husband was still in Hawaii. It was Saturday, June 19, 1964, the day before Father's Day. In those days, they put us to sleep before the baby came. And, of course, we did not know what sex the baby was. At about four o'clock, I underwent anesthetic, and when I woke up they said, "Congratulations! You have a little boy!" I also remember my brother telling someone to get the spider off the headboard of the bed because I was deathly afraid of spiders. We had already decided on a name, Scott Allen Pape. Then we called my husband in Hawaii and wished him a happy Father's Day. At first, he didn't get it, but when he did, he began his trip home to meet his son.

On the first day I could visit the nursery to observe the infants in their bassinets, I heard a man behind me making fun of the fact that the names of the babies were written on Scott paper towels, and my baby's name was Scott Pape. I wanted to punch him!

When his grandma came to see him, the first thing she said to me was, "What is he going to do with those initials on his luggage when he goes to college?" At that point, I wasn't too concerned about it. Actually, from the time he joined a fraternity in college, all of the guys called him SAP, and nobody seemed to care. In fact, his two-year-old son is currently called SAP Jr., and that seems fine with all concerned.

All my husband's relatives from Milwaukee came up to see the baby. My mother had lunch and dinner guests every day for a week. Everybody had to hold him and pass him around. I was trying to nurse a baby and also entertain my in-laws. Unbeknownst to me, my parents and my husband would take Scott into the kitchen every night and give him bottled milk because they thought he wasn't getting enough to eat. This, of course, ruined my ability to nurse.

And then, after a week, my husband and all the company left. Scott started to experience projectile vomiting and had to go back into the hospital. Once again, my mother became hysterical. Finally, the doctor told me I could not bring her to the hospital.

By the time Scott was a month old and I flew back to San Diego with him in his infant seat, I began to wonder if it wouldn't have been less chaotic if I had just stayed in San Diego to give birth. The airline stewardesses were wonderful. In those days, they had small pull-down holders in the front of the airplane, and I could put the baby in there to sleep. They didn't have the combination infant seats and strollers like they have today. But I got used to traveling alone with a baby. I would do it several times in the next few years, before we finally moved back to Chicago in January 1966, when our second child, Debbie, was born. Scott was a real trooper, and everyone always commented, "What a pretty baby!" And he was handsome, indeed.

IT'S A GIRL!

"Let me time those contractions," my husband said as he held his watch under the lamp so he could see better.

"I've done this once before, and I know there's no time to spare!" I said, my voice raising with anxiety. "Get Scott down to the Guzemans and put my suitcase in the car and let's get going. It feels like the baby's sitting between my knees."

We rushed to Copley Hospital. I was helped into a wheelchair and went up in the elevator. It was 5:00 AM on Friday, February 24, 1966, and I awoke out of a sound sleep with labor pains and my water broken. When we called Dr. Blackwell, he couldn't believe it was going that fast, and so he took his time getting there. My husband rode up in the elevator with him, recognizing him only because I had described him as an extremely large, overweight man. All his patients loved him because he never got on us about gaining too much weight.

I still had two black velvet bows in my hair that I had forgotten to remove last night. The nurses took me to the delivery room and were scurrying around. Again, these were the days where we were totally drugged with anesthetic and woke up to find out the sex and size of the baby. There was no ultrasound like there is today.

I tried to figure out why everyone kept saying "but" or, as I realized later, "butt." My baby was being born breech. I had just been to the doctor that week, but it wasn't discovered. When the doctor arrived, he was shocked at how far along I was (already dilated to ten centimeters). He gave me a local anesthetic, asked if I could feel anything, cut two times, and then said, "It's a girl!" I do remember them rolling a baby with fairly dark hair, wrapped in towels, by me, and then they gave me an anesthetic, and I don't remember anything more. Later, the doctor said to me, "If you ever decide to have a third child, just call me and I'll stop by. You're the fastest delivery I've had!"

We had already decided on the name Debra. I had decided that with my friend Judy Meyers, remember? And we were thrilled to have a girl and a boy. I knew I was done.

On Sunday morning, after finding out we had no insurance, they told me I could go home. I was able to get back into my regular clothes, and we headed back to our home at 430 Grand Avenue in Aurora, Illinois.

A NEW CHRISTMAS RITUAL

It is Christmas Day. Most of the country sits down to a fancy dinner of turkey, dressing, and cranberry, served on a white linen tablecloth in the formal dining room. My two kids and I hang out around the kitchen table, two fondue pots and several dips and condiments in the bowls on the table. Long fondue forks stick up out of their wooden holders. Hot grease boils in the red pot, while the candle warmer underneath the pot keeps it hot. We stab chunks of raw beef on our fondue forks and put them into the grease. We hear the sizzle as they begin to cook, and we smell the aroma of cooking beef. One rare, one medium and one well done; we each cook the meat exactly the way we like it. And then we dip it into the hot chili sauce dip or the curried mayonnaise or even into the second pot, with melted cheddar cheese fondue. We dip pieces of French bread in the cheese. My mouth waters as I think about it.

When we finally are stuffed full of beef, cheese, and bread, we are ready for a special treat: chocolate fondue for dessert. We dip strawberries, pear pieces, apple slices, marshmallows, and pieces of pound cake. Melted cooking chocolate, German sweet chocolate, and chocolate chips combine to tickle our taste buds.

Several years after the divorce, the kids spent one Christmas Day and night with their dad, and I decided that I wasn't going to do a "formal Christmas dinner" on the twenty-sixth, so we fondued by candlelight, with "Silent Night" playing on the stereo. We liked it so much that we adopted this ritual for the next dozen or so years. I chuckled when my daughter brought her fiancé home to meet me and we sat down to fondue. I realized how traditional he was when his eyes almost popped out at the sight of the fondue pots.

"Where's the turkey?" he asked, looking astonished. And I explained our tradition.

I also chuckled last Christmas when I visited my daughter, her husband, and my grandkids. Once again, we sat around the kitchen table, with fondue pots on the table, and "Silent Night" on the CD player! Will wonders never cease? We sure had a good time.

CHRISTMAS AT THE PAPES

One of our traditions was to put together a one-hundred-piece jigsaw puzzle on Christmas Eve before church at 11:00 PM. Part of our reason for doing this was to help us to stay awake. We liked the tradition so much that we continued doing it long after we switched to the early service.

"Look, Ma, my cranberry jelly jelled!" My daughter just had to rub it in. The last few years, my jelly poured off the plate! I used the same recipe that my mother had used for years, putting the skins through the Foley Food Mill and boiling the cranberries on the stove. But no matter what I did, I couldn't make it jell. But Debbie could, and she wanted a picture of it for posterity.

One of our favorite things was the Santa Claus we put up in the backyard. In fact, my neighbors at Wheaton Oaks always comment on how much they enjoy the decorations behind my town house. The kids can sit at the kitchen table and look right out the window at Santa.

In front of the house, I love the luminary candles. My grandson Matthew and I put these up several years ago, and we all enjoyed them a lot.

FOR THE MOTHER WHO HAS EVERYTHING

"Merry Christmas, Mom!" Both Scott and Debbie were sitting on my bed at six o'clock on Christmas morning 1988. They handed me a huge card, which read on the envelope, *For the mother who has everything.*

I opened the card, and we took off on a treasure hunt: looking under the bed; heading down to the basement and looking in the dryer; going up into the kitchen and looking in the oven; proceeding into the family room and looking behind the television console—and finally the last clue led me behind the wet bar in the downstairs family room. And there it was—an orangutan! My two kids were laughing hysterically. Among the giggles, they managed to tell me they had gone out to Toys "R" Us the night before, on Christmas Eve, and found the monstrous stuffed animal. It had cost a fortune, but they thought it was worth it.

Over the last fifteen years, this animal has lived in the basement of our Aurora office, where one of our renters found it sitting in his client chair and called me to see if it was okay to move it. Finally, in 2005, I sent it to Debbie for Christmas. What do they say? "What goes around comes around!"

JOINING THE TWENTY-FIRST CENTURY

"Hey, Ma, " my son always used to chide me, "why don't you join the twenty-first century?"

What he is referring to is the fact that, up until about five years ago, I didn't know how to use a computer, a cell phone (including retrieving a voice mail), or anything else that reeked of technology.

So I called my computer consultant/church friend and said, "Fred, the time has come: I *have* to start learning how to use the computer." It doesn't work to read the books—I have tried that before, and my brain just doesn't work that way. When my kids were little, I used to put together their toys on Christmas Eve, and there would always be extra screws and whatnot, which I just threw away. The directions only confused me.

I would spend my first half hour of each day experimenting with different programs such as Word—not WordPerfect because no one could open it. My office manager is a whiz on the computer and on all things technological in general. Each time I would have a success—"Hey, Lauren, I just sent an attachment and they actually *got* it."—she would be my cheerleader: "Yay!"

My granddaughter has lived with me during her college breaks, and I believe that her cell phone is attached to her ear. I told her I never use one, and she just rolled her eyes and said, "Oh, Grandma."

Since I pick her up at the bus in Oakbrook Shopping Mall, and since there are about thirty buses, it has motivated me to learn how to use the cell phone. I was so excited the first time I was able to find her in front of Macy's. When I dialed her number, she said, "Grandma, I'm right in front of you!" And she was. I was so proud of myself. Last time she was home, I even figured out how to retrieve her voice mail: "Grandma, I missed my bus, and I'll be seven hours late." I sure was glad I figured out how to do that, instead of getting there and her not being there.

Now I really love the things I am learning. What used to intimidate me now intrigues me. I can send and receive e-mails from my eight-year-old grandson in California, I am able to communicate on Facebook with my granddaughter and her roommate, and I do believe that I have finally "joined the twenty-first century."

GRANDCHILDREN

I'M A GRANDMA!

"If anyone had told me ten years ago that I would be sitting here on this dais with the bishop of the Evangelical Lutheran Church in America, the synod bishop from California, the women leaders in the synod, and celebrating the Decade of Women's Ordination, I would have laughed out loud! I started as a church secretary in 1973, making three dollars an hour, working thirty-three hours a week. I think I've come a long way, with God's help and guidance." That's what I said when they asked me to contribute a few words to the opening ceremony.

We were worried if the women clergy would sign up for the half-hour counseling sessions with me. I put the sign-up sheet on my door, and by the time I went to dinner and the opening worship service, it was full! And that continued for all four days and evenings. There were women clergy from around the world, so the diversity of clothing, languages, ethnicity, worship, and music was amazing. We snake-danced, administered communion to each other, anointed each other with oil, and shared our stories and experiences we had as women. Such a glorious time!

* * *

Lamaze was something I also never expected to attend at the age of fifty years! So when Scott, his wife, and I were sitting listening to the instructions about how to breathe, relax, and push, I was in a brand-new world.

"What is this?" she shrieked as water gushed all over the floor where we were sitting.

"It's time to go to the hospital," I said. "Go get the car, Scott."

It was a short ride to Sharp Memorial Hospital. I looked up once and realized Scott was about to hit a kid on a bicycle while he hovered over his wife. "Watch out!" I hollered, and he veered the car to the left and avoided the boy.

We settled into a birthing room. She was pretty scared, and there wasn't much we could do for her. The epidural helped, and she and

Scott began their all-night vigil and birthing process. I finally went out into the lobby to lie down for a few minutes.

"You're a grandma," I heard my son say as he shook me awake. It's a healthy girl: Brittany Nicole Pape. Come and hold her." I was so excited. She was beautiful, with blond hair and blue eyes. I had forgotten how tiny newborns are.

The next day, I went to the Hallmark store and loaded up on all things pink (balloons, streamers, signs, toys, bibs, clothes, and whatever else I could stuff in my bag). By the time Brittany and her mother came home, it looked like a pink party land. I'd even found a Madame Alexander doll named "Nicole" and wrapped that up for her.

Brittany's aunt Debbie came to see her, as well as some other friends. Scott asked if I would mind babysitting while they went down to the pool. Mind? Oh my gosh, it was wonderful. I have told Brittany that this was my first "feminist" conversation with my first granddaughter. Oh, how I hoped to have some influence with her and to be able to pass along some of the wisdom I had gained through my experience of fifty years.

The following is my journal entry from the day Brittany was born:

7/16/90

My dearest Brittany,

Welcome! What a special time for me to be in San Diego with your mom and dad at the time—two weeks early, at that—when you chose to make your appearance into the world. I hope you will fill your life with surprises of your own choosing.

Although I struggled terribly with approaching the age of fifty and the idea of being a grandmother, all I had to do was hold you and look into those beautiful blue eyes to know that it would be okay—that

I was going to cherish the time I would spend with you and the opportunity to watch your personhood and your life unfold.

I have just spent three wonderful days in Los Angeles with five hundred Lutheran clergywomen celebrating twenty years of women being ordained in the ministry. I listened to their personal and professional struggles and victories during the last two decades. As I sat on the platform with our ELCA bishop, the keynote speaker, and the chair of the conference, I was filled with awe and wonder at the events in my own life in the last twenty years. In front of the group (I was serving as the on-site therapist during the conference, so aptly titled *Stirring Up the Nest*), I spoke about how we surely have "come a long way, baby!" I spoke of the year 1974–75, when I was employed as the parish secretary for three dollars per hour, ninety-nine dollars per week, and how I believed at that time that it probably was about as far as I would ever go. If anyone had told me I would be sitting on the dais at a clergywomen's conference, I would have said the person was crazy.

And so, my dear Brittany, my message to you is to dream big!

The whole conference was filled with celebration: of being a woman, of serving others, of transforming anger, bitterness, and helplessness into opportunity, empowerment, and self-actualization.

I didn't realize how happy I would be to find out that my first grandchild was a little girl, born during a time of so much celebration and opportunities for women.

When you were two days old, your parents, Aunt Debbie, and other friends who had stopped by to welcome you were down cooking dinner by the pool. I babysat for the first time, and we had our first "woman-to-woman" talk. Actually, you slept calmly on my shoulder, and I was telling you how thrilled and delighted I was with you, and how I hoped I would be the kind of grandmother or role model or mentor you needed and wanted. And so we began our relationship together.

10/16/90

I got a chance to spend time with you when you were just three months old. Your parents celebrated their anniversary, and I stayed with you. I was so worried I would not hear you at night, so I slept with my head a foot from your crib. It was just fine. We both got up at 5:00 AM. You're such a cheerful morning person, just like I am. Early mornings are such a wonderful time of day, aren't they? You're such a good baby, and I do so love being with you. To smile at you and to have you smile back at me is so wonderful. You are loved, dear Brittany, and you don't need to do anything but just be you.

2/17/91

You are now one of God's baptized children, and all your family and friends were happy to be with you for this happy occasion. As I was in Marshall Fields, getting your baptismal dress, I found myself bragging about you to anyone who would listen. I realized I had joined the "Proud Grandma Club."

4/16/91

Lo and behold, you're now living with us! You are nine months old, full of life, energy, curiosity, all those wonderful traits of the young. I hope you will never lose these qualities, for they continue forever to make life exciting. I love to watch and play with you. It is wonderful to watch you enjoy life so much; don't ever lose that capacity, my dear Brittany, because life truly is enjoyable. It is simply up to each of us to enjoy it.

5/16/91

As I sit in my hotel room in Portland, Oregon, I think of you, with your whole life ahead of you, and it makes me pause to look at my own life as a woman in the twentieth century. My own fifty-year journey has had its ups and downs, but it has been such a learning time. Perhaps I will be able to share some of it with you.

The thought that came to me this morning was related to what I have learned during this journey about my "ticket to happiness," or success, and how that has changed over time. I was reflecting on my own growing-up years, with a father who was very successful by society's standards (president of a company, good income, nice home); and of my mother, who was also successful in her prescribed role (dependent financially and emotionally on my father, social, and friendly). Everybody loved Helen Grover! And where I fit into all this role-modeling ...

I remember June 27, 1962, when I married your Grandpa Pape. I believed that this was my ticket to happiness, and that if I was a good navy wife and pleasing to others, I would find happiness.

In the sixties, it did not seem to matter what my strengths and weaknesses were as a person, only that I fulfilled my role as wife and mother. So I did. I sometimes wondered why I went to college at Northwestern University, and why my father had expectations that I get good grades (As and Bs). On the other hand, it was also expected that I get married as soon as I graduated (I did that one really well, only three days later). I was also supposed to be trained as a teacher, just in case I ever needed to work ... a backup. This was my only rebellion: I refused to get an education degree.

I still remember my father's view of social workers: they trudged around in the slums of Chicago, and they were never safe. So I did what any respectable young girl would do: got married and moved to San Diego, California.

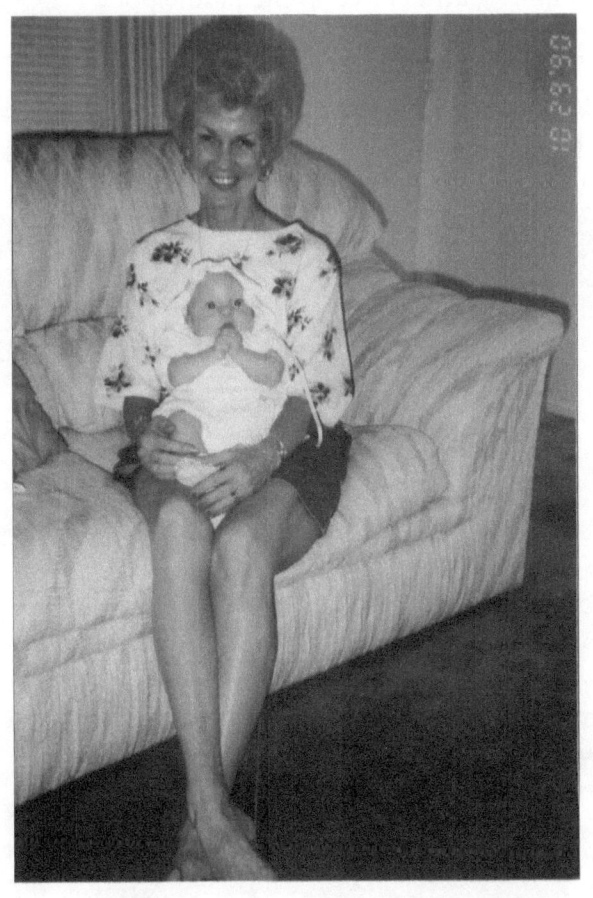

MY BIRTHDAY AT LAKE GENEVA

The pictures say it all! We had such fun. Brittany is three, and Breanna is one. They are both so affectionate and loving, and I felt simply ecstatic to spend my fifty-third birthday this way.

We walked, talked, and played in the kiddie pool. I hope we can do this every year!

The birthday cake was my favorite: white cake with white frosting. I didn't need any other presents besides these two little girls.

SPECIAL DELIVERY

My suitcase was lying open on the basement floor, half-filled, and clothes hung overhead on the water pipe. Matthew was due to arrive in one week, October 21, 1998, and I could hardly contain my excitement. I walked through the baby department at the Target down the road daily, picking up one more item—a rattle, another bib, a tiny basketball, a Michael Jordan Bulls outfit—and carefully packed each of them in my suitcase.

I'd wake up full of anticipation in the middle of the night. I dreamed about baby boys. I worried that I might faint during the delivery. I worked hard not to talk to everyone, all of the time, about my daughter's expected first baby.

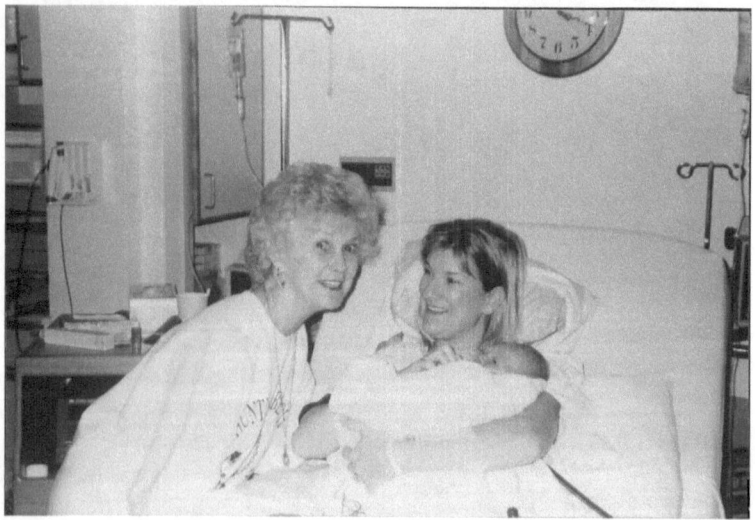

On October 14, I went to work as usual. As a psychotherapist, I had several clients to see that day, including a new couple at 4:00 PM. When I answered a phone call at 3:00 PM, my daughter announced, "My water broke; we're on the way to the hospital!" My hands started shaking, my heart was racing, tears came to my eyes, and I said, "I'm on my way!"

I convinced the ticket agent I *had* to be on the next flight to Anaheim, California. I will never forget running out the front door as my new young couple arrived, saying, "I'm so sorry; we'll have to reschedule; my daughter is having a baby!" I rushed home, threw my clothes into the suitcase, and jumped into the limousine.

I usually sleep on the four-hour flight, but this night I couldn't even close my eyes. Everyone sitting even remotely close to me knew my daughter was having her first baby. The man sitting next to me finally put on his earphones and closed his eyes. I took the hint. I kept quiet.

The L.A. airport was busy for 11:00 PM. Flashing lights from the airplanes twinkled through the glass. Moving carts beeped, warning us to get out of their way. Two hundred passengers, yawning and sleepy-eyed, waited for their luggage. I grabbed my suitcase and ran to wave down a taxi.

The director of ground services hailed me a cab and instructed the driver to go to St. Joseph Hospital. My daughter had assured me that it was the biggest hospital in the area and *everyone* knew where it was. Everyone except me. And the cabdriver. He was Chinese, did not speak much English, had no idea where the hospital was, and just stared at me with a blank look on his face. He had beady brown eyes and a mustache and wore one of those brown flat cloth hats like Chicagoans wear in the winter.

After three long minutes of trying to communicate with the driver, my patience was gone, my chest and stomach were tight, and I wanted to scream. I jumped out of the cab and told the man in charge to get me another cab. "No, no," he said. "I'll give him instructions, and we'll get you there right away." I got back in the cab, and suddenly we shot forward and took off.

As he pulled up in front of the hospital, I leaped out, dragging my heavy suitcase into the entrance. "Which room is Debra Pape in?" I asked breathlessly. "She's having a baby!"

The nurse, dressed in a white pantsuit, with cold blue eyes, blond hair, and no smile, said sarcastically, "This *is* the maternity ward. I'm sorry, but we don't have a Debra Pape."

By now, I had had it. In a forced controlled tone, through clenched teeth, I said, "Look again. She's here!"

The nurse sighed, banged the name in the keyboard again, and said, "Look, like I told you, there is no Debra Pape."

Then I realized … "Oh my gosh!" My face reddened. I felt hot, and I quietly said, "I'm so sorry. It's Debra Skjerven. Pape is her maiden name."

The nurse rolled her eyes and said, "Follow me," leading me to the room I gently opened the door. All I could see in the dark was a beige cloth screen. There was no noise—just silence. Then I heard a weak, "Mom?"

"Oh, yes," I said, my heart in my throat. I walked around the screen, trying not to run.

My daughter was sitting up in the bed, a huge grin on her face. She handed me a tiny bundle, wrapped in a soft blue flannel blanket, and said, "Meet your new grandson, Matthew!"

DID JESUS HAVE A GRANDMA?

It's the first Sunday of Advent. I just mailed out my last Christmas card and my Christmas letter. In it, I referred to the fact that my daughter is expecting her second child, Mark, and the due date is January 6, 2001, but that we are pretty sure it will be a Christmas baby.

More and more of my activities are taking place with an eye toward that "Christmas child" I am so anxiously awaiting. I am wrapping all my Christmas gifts and will send them out tomorrow to California a bit early, just in case … My suitcase is partially packed, lying open on the basement floor. I have alerted all my clients that sometime in the next thirty days I will get that phone call that I am so eagerly awaiting: "The baby is coming! Head for California!" I will spend a week out there, taking care of two-year-old Matthew, my daughter, and the new baby. My backup therapists are in place, and all preparations are done.

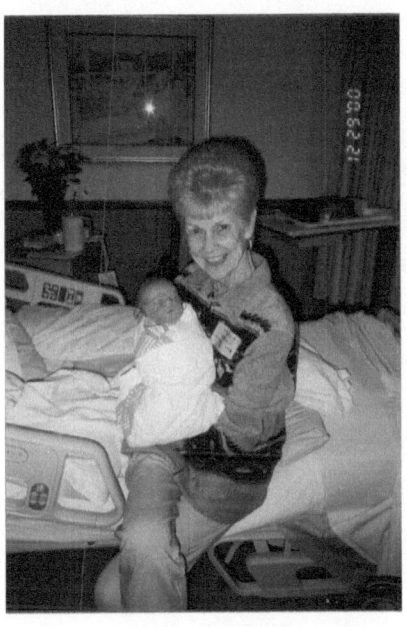 

More and more of my thoughts are focused on the anticipated blessed event—that miracle of birth: the excitement that fills the room as the first sight of the baby's head appears; the love of family as we first hold the newborn; the multitude of pictures taken, to be stored away in albums for future memories and reminiscing. Tears come to my eyes as I remember past births and imagine what this one will be like. What a special gift from God!

And then suddenly, out of nowhere (and yet I know it is out of "somewhere"—from God), the analogy hit me. I have never entered into the Advent season expecting and waiting for a "real" baby. And what if I thought and felt and planned my entire life around the anticipation of the Christ child, like I am doing with my awaited grandchild? What if I allowed the feelings of anticipation, joy, and happiness about this "real" baby, who will be born two thousand miles from here, to extend to the Christ child who was born two thousand years ago, on the other side of the world? What if I "held" the Christ child in my arms and allowed all the love that I already know I will feel to be fully expressed toward the babe in the manger? How would my life be different? What impact would this have?

Did Jesus have a Grandma who patiently (or impatiently) waited, prayed for Mary and Joseph, and increasingly centered her life activities around being ready for the baby's birth? If Jesus *did* have a grandma, then she was truly blessed, as only a grandma can be. The love of a grandma for her grandchildren is truly special, a miracle from God. This Advent season, as I await my yet-to-be-born grandchild, I am grateful to God for this holy insight.

HERNIAS, DOUBLE HERNIAS, AND MATCHING BLUE HATS

We were the only two people sitting in the hospital cafeteria, drinking coffee and trying not to be anxious. Our one-year-old daughter, Debbie, was up in surgery for a hernia. Suddenly, the phone rang, clear across the room but so loud it sounded like the bell at a boxing match. We jumped up, and my husband ran over to answer it. *Surely it can't be for us,* I thought. But sure enough, my husband called me over to the phone. The voice on the phone identified herself as the assisting nurse in surgery.

"Which side was your daughter's hernia on? The doctor wrote down the right, and the nurse wrote down the left."

What? I can't believe it! I thought. "It is on her right side," I said. *It's a good thing mothers pay attention!*

I went over and sat down. Now we really were nervous. It didn't seem possible that just a week ago I had discovered a lump the size of a golf ball in Debbie's lower abdomen. Each time I pushed it back in, it seemed to stay, so I didn't think much about it. Then a few days ago she had a well-baby checkup, and I told the pediatrician about the lump. Of course, he wanted to see it. And, of course, it wouldn't come back out. So he said to take her home and make her walk around until it came back out. Then bring her in immediately. So I did.

He told me he had never seen such a big hernia in a one-year-old. It was the size of a five-year-old's hernia. I scheduled the surgery immediately. It was to be done on Good Friday. So that year Debbie had her Easter bonnet and her Easter basket in her crib in Copley Hospital. The surgery went fine, but in some ways it was a foreboding of some of the unusual accidents she would have in the future. It probably was just as well I didn't know then what I know now.

In 2003, Mark, Debbie's second son, was diagnosed with a double hernia, and surgery was scheduled for September. I flew out to help them with Matthew. When Mark came home from the hospital, he brought his blue paper surgical hat. How he loved to wear the hat and play "surgery." I remember teaching him how to put on his blue surgical hat, lie on the couch, and moan ever so slightly.

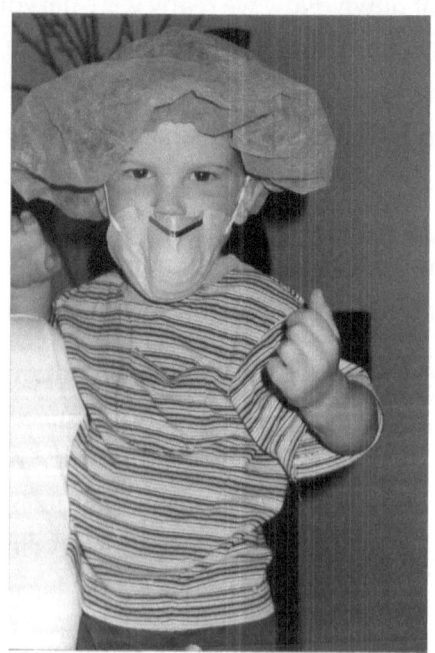

This brought immediate attention from anyone in the room ... and usually some ice cream or something good to drink. He was up and running around in no time.

In February 2008, I was scheduled for lung cancer surgery, and my daughter was with me as I was getting ready to go into the operating room. Of course, I too received my little blue paper surgical hat. Mark had sent a message with his mother: "I want a picture of Nanee in her blue paper hat!"

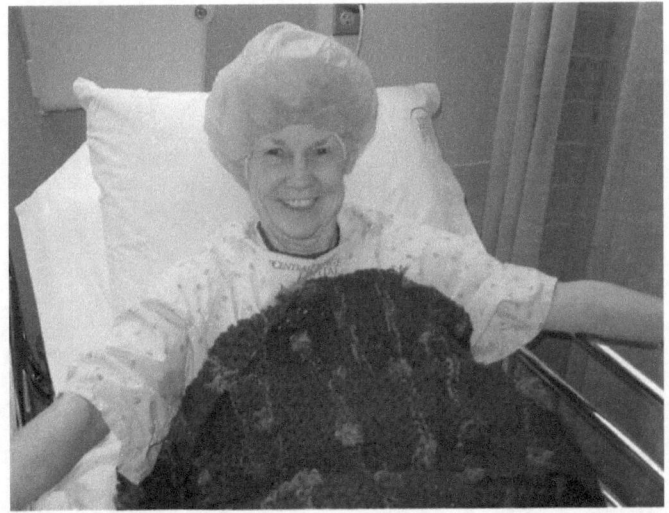

In this day of technology, Debbie was able not only to take a picture, but also to send it immediately to Mark, who was at the other end. My surgery also was successful, and so to this day, I enjoy our pictures of our blue matching hats!

UPS HATS AND TRUCKS

Every Christmas, I send two huge boxes by United Parcel Service to my daughter and her family in California. Many of the gifts are for my two- and four-year-old grandsons.

Last year, Matthew, then three, ran as fast as he could into the house, yelling to my daughter as the UPS truck rolled up in front of the house, "Mommy, Mommy, here comes Nanee's truck!"

PAPE CHRISTMASES—
A SPECIAL TIME OF YEAR

Christmas Eve Service

Stuffing the turkey
Christmas Eve

Santa Claus "Jr."

She is born!

ADVENT CALENDAR TRADITION

For the last four decades, our family has observed the tradition that on each Thanksgiving, every child and grandchild gets an Advent calendar, with windows to open each day of Advent. Some have stickers, like the picture above, and some are fancier, with drawers, like the one below. Either way, it has been a longtime tradition that has provided us with lots of fun. Usually they are stuck up on the refrigerator, and we open them first thing in the morning.

GRANDKIDS

Mark Skjerven, Stephen Mercado, David Mercado, Scott Pape, Jr., Brittany Pape, George Mercado, Breanna Pape, Matthew Skjerven, Jenna Pape

Look at those wonderful, unique kids! I got this bracelet for my birthday August 2, 2009, and it is so special. I have important memories from each of these kids.

Matthew, Mark, and the beach in California rank high on my list. And the pranks they pull and the jokes they play … We laugh a lot.

Christmas memories are important with Stephen, David, and George: stockings, singing, dancing animals, and lots of fun.

Unique to the girls are a couple of trips to see *The Nutcracker*, the celebration of Three Kings' Day (Epiphany), and my fifty-third birthday celebration at my condo at The Abbey, in Wisconsin.

Scott, Jr., is the cutest little one: full of energy, big hazel eyes, fun laugh, and curious about everything. He loves the wind chimes.

I look forward to future events, trips, birthdays, and holidays with all these young ones. Perhaps I can share some of the things I have learned over the years, but probably they will have to learn these things for themselves. I will just be here to support and love them.

PROFESSIONAL JOURNEY

RIDING A BICYCLE

"Hold on tight. Focus straight ahead. Hold your head up high. And go!" my father yelled as he let go of the bicycle. I was six years old, and the training wheels had just been taken off of my little red and blue bicycle. I say "little," looking back at my memory of the bicycle. It was as tall as I was, about three feet, and at the time, it seemed enormous. My father was teaching me how to ride. I remember him holding the back of the seat, and I felt secure when his hand was there. Then he said "I'm going to let go. You can do it!" I felt a knot in the pit of my stomach. Fear? Excitement? I loved the feeling of the wind blowing in my face, dragging my long blond curls back away from my cheeks. I shrieked in delight. This reminded me of sledding in Phillips Park with my father.

"Do it again!" I yelled back to him. And he did. He practiced with me until I learned how to ride my two-wheeler. And I always felt safe when I knew he was close enough to grab the bike if I started to fall.

Riding a bicycle was a little like starting my career: fearful and exciting.

* * *

"You can do it," Alice said. It was 1976, and I was employed by my church, St. Paul Lutheran Church, as the church secretary. I was a single parent, made three dollars per hour, and worked a maximum of thirty-three hours per week. Not much to support two kids who loved to eat. I had been searching for jobs in the social work field (I had my BA in sociology from Northwestern University), and everyone kept telling me I would need a master's degree in social work to get the jobs I was looking for. A master's degree? My grades weren't that good from undergraduate school. *I can't ever do that,* I said to myself. Although I sure wanted to.

My job at the church consisted of answering phones, doing the church bulletins for each Sunday, and anything else the pastor wanted me to do. Most weeks this took about twenty hours, and I was left with many extra hours. So I volunteered to be the Sunday School superintendent, the vacation Bible school director, the nursery coordinator, and the president of the Lutheran Women's Group. I loved starting new projects and coming up with creative ideas (I had no idea at the time that this was part of being an entrepreneur, which would become central to my life later on).

Mary Ann Wanucha, an employee from the Divisionary of the DuPage County Probation Department, came to present an educational program for our adult forum at church. She talked about their work with adolescents, keeping kids out of court and doing family therapy with the families of the kids in trouble. It sounded just like something I would love. The question was how to get from the church secretary's chair to the family therapist's chair?

"Is this Pat Pape?" the voice asked.

"Yes," I said hesitantly.

"This is Mary Ann Wanucha. I was at your church several months ago, talking about our diversionary program.

"Oh, yes," I said excitedly.

"Well, we have had a position of secretary open up, and we wondered if you would be interested. It's full time with benefits, and it pays fifteen thousand dollars."

"Can I get back to you tomorrow?" I asked.

"Sure, that's fine."

I called my friend Alice and asked her what I should do. I remember her words: "Pat, this is really a no-brainer! Three times as much money, and you will be at an agency where they're doing what you love to do. What's to think about?"

"I don't know if I can work full time, take care of my kids … and I also want to go to graduate school for my MSW."

"You'll find a way," she said.

And I did. Transformative moment? You betcha. It was a little like learning to ride a bicycle. I loved the thrill in the pit of my stomach. If I think about it, I do believe my father gave me the yearning that he also had, to take risks and accept challenges. The difference between us was that *I took them.*

FAMILY DIVERSION DIVISION

Ed Engel, Mary Ann Wanucha, Shirley Lindquist, Pat McGrath,
Pat Pape, Gary Balgemann, Vi Lowe, and Don Perardi

By 1977, I was accepted by George Williams College in Downers Grove, Illinois, to start working toward my master's degree in social work. But for the moment, I was still doing work for the therapists, seated behind my typewriter at the Diversionary Division of the DuPage County Probation Department. I had mastered this job and did it well, but I *yearned* to be doing family therapy with the other staff. I listened to the client families come in, often arguing or discussing their differences. I would try to imagine what I would suggest they do to resolve their problems. Everyone at work knew that my dream was to become a family counselor one day, and they included me in all of their training sessions. I read everything I could get my hands on, in order to learn more about families and family therapy, especially as it related to working with Minors in Need of Supervision (MINS) cases. I kept watching from behind my typewriter.

* * *

"Would you like to be a family therapist?" I heard the low, engaging voice of my boss, Ed Engel. I looked up from my typewriter and saw his deep brown eyes and his huge, inviting smile.

"What are you talking about? Are you kidding? You know that is my ideal job," I replied.

He just kept smiling and said, "Nancy, one of our counselors, is leaving, and I need to replace her. Since the job description does not require a master's degree, I thought I would offer it to you first, before opening it up to the public."

I practically ran to the family therapy office that Nancy had occupied. I had butterflies in my stomach (excitement or fear?). All I could say was, "Absolutely I would!" And two weeks later, I started my new job. I trained Shirley to do my secretarial job, and she started immediately. And so I started a new pattern that would last until June 1979: four ten-hour days of work and two or three days of school. Since the faculty at my MSW program counted my time at work as an internship (both work and school were wonderfully accommodating), I was able to complete the complicated schedule.

My two kids got better grades than they ever had. I was getting straight As. We would celebrate good grades with steak dinners for all of us. And we always designated times when we would sit down to dinner together and share our days.

My first case as a family therapist is one I will never forget. A teenage girl was being dragged in by her father, while her mother, in her fur coat, stood watching. My friend Mary had stopped by and was just leaving. I ran after her, "Mary, please stay so I am not alone right now!" She came back in and sat down in one of the empty offices. I talked with the family and told them I would find alternative housing for their daughter until they could go to court the next day and figure out the best arrangements for her. I called Pat, my supervisor, and said, "I will take her to my house."

She didn't mince any words. "You will do no such thing. First of all, it is illegal, and you will get arrested for kidnapping. Second of all, it is against our policies. Find her a temporary foster family." And so I learned a good lesson about appropriate professional boundaries. And also that I cannot save the world by myself.

I learned so much and felt so supported by the three other family therapists, Gary, Don, and Pat; our community resources coordinator, Mary Ann Wanucha; our secretary Shirley; and most of all my outstanding boss, Ed Engel, whom I credit with giving me the opportunity to begin my professional career.

The Diversionary Division, a three-year grant program, did not continue. But several years later, when I saw Ed in a restaurant and went flying across the room to give him a hug and say thank you, he simply blushed and looked shy and embarrassed. That was his manner, and he simply did not see anything particularly unusual about what he did. But I did, and I still do. I know God works through ordinary people to do extraordinary things. As my friend Tom says, "There are so many GMCs (God-manipulated coincidences) in your life!" And he is right.

THE ABBEY ALCOHOLISM
TREATMENT CENTER*

Luule Vess, Pat Pape, Carl Alaimo, Heather Hurley

The Abbey Alcoholism Treatment Center opened on Monday, June 2, 1980. It is the first freestanding center in the state of Illinois.

The Abbey provides an intensive, family-oriented 26-day residential treatment program for a maximum of 32 patients. Also offered are a comprehensive outpatient program for up to 150 persons, a weekly community education seminar series, and outreach programs for business and industry.

"The use of a family modality is the most promising way of treating alcoholism," said Director Patricia A. Pape, MSW, CSW, CADC. Pape, a family therapist and former resource development coordinator for DuPage County Diversionary Division, received training in alcoholism counseling at Loretto Hospital. Carl James Alaimo, MS, is the clinical coordinator of The Abbey, formerly of Mercy Hospital in Chicago.

Located on an estate surrounded by natural wooded beauty, The Abbey provides positive comfortable living for the patients as well as nutritional meals, in an atmosphere of serenity.

*Taken from a brochure describing the facility

GIVING BIRTH TO MY BUSINESS

I can't believe it, I thought. *Here I am being interviewed for my job as director of The Abbey Alcoholism Treatment Program.*

It was Friday, October 31, 1981, and I was sitting behind a desk in a small counseling office. Across from me was the vice president of the hospital that was buying the treatment program that I directed, and another hospital administrator. David was conducting the interview.

David simply stared at me with his deep brown eyes, and his good looks and charm were apparent, even at this difficult time. "Now don't be nervous," he reassured me. "This will all turn out fine."

* * *

I suddenly flashed back to the time a year and a half ago, when I'd decided to test the limits of our agreement with the hospital. David, the vice president of the hospital, had agreed they were to provide medical attention to our patients if needed, with priority being given to them. I took one of our patients to the ER, and they had put the patient and me in the cast room, where I had been sitting for over an hour. I finally called upstairs, reached David, and told him I was taking our patient to another hospital. Two minutes later, he stepped off the elevator and came over to see how he could help me. "What can I do?" he asked.

I said, "It's a little late. I just made arrangements to take this woman to another hospital."

He wasn't happy. He had lost a patient. Neither was I. He had broken our agreement to give priority treatment to our patients.

David asked me a few questions about my goals for the future. Then he and the other administrator got up and walked across the hallway into another room. Five, ten, fifteen minutes went by. When David walked back into the office, my heart sank. My breathing was shallow and fast. I held my hands so they wouldn't shake, and I spoke slowly to contain my anxiety. David gave me the news. "We have decided to bring in Park Side Medical Corporation, on a two-year management agreement, to run the program. You're welcome to stay on as a counselor, under their director and their program."

I was devastated! "But I wrote and directed the program for The Abbey. It's a wonderful program, and we were helping families to recover. And besides, you promised you would keep me on as the director of the new program if I held it together while you completed the purchase." I felt helpless and hopeless as I sat there. David gave no indication that he was going to say anything further, and I didn't know what to say. His appearance was cold and uncaring. I realized they had no intention of keeping their verbal agreement. David stood up, offered me his hand, and asked me to let him know if I wanted to stay or leave. That was a pretty easy decision: I told him I was leaving. As I turned to walk out of the room, I could feel the anger beginning to well up in me. I walked slowly down the long, dark hallway to the staff who had stayed to support me. They just hugged me and told me I would be okay. At some level, I knew that. It's just that this was my dream job, with a dream salary, that I thought I would be doing until I retired, some thirty years later.

* * *

The eighteen months of my employment with The Abbey had been exciting at times, stressful at others. In May 1980, Charlie and Bob asked me if I would accept a position with them to write and direct the first freestanding alcoholism treatment program in DuPage County. I always believed in what I was doing. Charlie was the spiritual one, even at the end. He kept assuring us "God will provide," even as our paychecks kept bouncing. We later found out that none of the patients were being billed. As the administrator, Charlie should have supervised the billing of patients. Bob was the financial backer, and he ended up losing everything. He was older, partially balding, more cautious, and not so trusting as Charlie was.

I was at my best when I was working with client families. Every Thursday night was family night, and eight families were gathered in the group room. My heart beat with excitement because this was my favorite work. Some of the family members looked at the floor, others stared at their hands, and some glared at me because they didn't want to be there. I knew from experience that by the end of the two hours of experiential work, they would be in a very different place.

"Pick someone you don't know, from a family other than your own, and find out three things about that person so you can introduce him to the group," I said. I could feel the energy in the room begin to build. I loved this feeling: anticipation, curiosity, wonderment.

After the introductions, the clients felt more comfortable with each other and chatted more informally, making eye contact and laughing together.

Then I gave them their assignment for the next hour. They would work as a family, at their own table, with the paper, markers, scissors, and cardboard they had been given. They were to build a house. Their only rule was that they could not talk to each other until the house was done.

They tried to use nonverbal communication. The person with the most power in the family would be easy to spot: everyone looked to him or her for permission before they did anything. Kids might giggle when their parents couldn't figure out what to do next. I simply walked around and observed.

"Okay! Time's up!" I hollered. "How was that for you? What did you learn about you or your family members? Who wants to share first?" I smiled, sounded upbeat, and awaited their insights.

"Everyone looked at Dad before they would do anything!" said one five-year-old boy.

"What does that mean, I wonder?" I asked.

"Probably everyone's afraid of Dad!" he answered.

"Is that true, do you think?" I asked Dad.

"Gosh, I never thought I was scary! Are you afraid of me?" he asked his son.

"Kind of, especially when you're drinking," he said quietly, looking at the floor.

And so the conversation continued, with family members sharing with each other to the extent they were able. I had already indicated rules that made this a safe place for all family members to share with each. That was my primary goal: a safe place.

This is the work that warms my heart. I may confront behaviors, but I think clients know that I genuinely care for them as human beings. My work feels like fun a lot of the time, and I love it.

* * *

Throughout the process of the hospital purchasing our treatment program, I remained strong. I showed no signs of emotion and continued to give words of encouragement to the staff, until the next to the last day. As I led the final staff meeting, tears started running down my eyes, out of my control, and my eyes kept getting redder and redder. Finally, one of the members of my staff took me over to the hospital ER, and they diagnosed conjunctivitis. Since all of us were therapists, we decided that this was psychosomatic: I needed to cry. It was later that I remembered the only other times I had conjunctivitis, two Christmas Days in my childhood. What was that connection? Was I that stressed when I was two and three years old? Were there people there to support me then, as there were in 1981?

I was moving into an unknown future: Halloween night of 1981 was the night I went home and saw my first private practice client, and it was the birth of my business, Pape & Associates, which is still a successful entity today.

TRANSITIONAL YEAR

I did not know it then, but on that Friday, Halloween night, 1981, as I walked away from my former job as director of The Abbey Alcoholism Treatment Center and home to see my first private client in my home, I began a year of major transition: from employee to self-employed entrepreneur.

The following Tuesday morning, I headed for the unemployment office in Villa Park, Illinois. As I walked in the front door, I was full of shame, for I had learned an important lesson from my father: *never take handouts from anyone, especially the government!* So I could picture him turning over in his grave. Then I heard a voice holler out, "Hey, Pat, what are *you* doing here?" I looked up and saw one of my former patients from the treatment center, front teeth knocked out in a barroom brawl, big smile on his face, and I wished I could disappear into the floor.

"Same thing you are, so let's just not talk about it, okay?" I said in a voice so low it sounded like a whisper.

"Okay," he said. "Just let me know if I can be of help." He looked like he would have loved the role reversal.

I finally got started with unemployment, which I ended up living on for one year. I did all of the required interviewing, but I just could not find a job that was what I wanted. I am sure part of the problem was that I had planned on having my former job until the day I retired.

My business office was in my basement, under the vents from the furnace that stretched across the ceiling to convey the heat. My "office" consisted of a round beige card table, a black push-button telephone, an answering machine, and two boxes of three-by-five-inch cards, one for clients and one for referral resources. Actually, I still have the boxes and still use them personally, although I do not tell my techie friends.

I always got depressed if I had nowhere to go, so every Monday and every Thursday, I booked luncheon appointments with professionals that I knew or that I wanted to know. And then I networked, networked, networked.

After a few months, when I had about twenty-five clients, I was comfortable meeting with them in the living room. We sat at ninety-degree angles so I could see down my hallway. One day, as I was counseling a gentleman who was on probation, I looked up in time to see my daughter, wrapped in a huge bath towel, with another towel turban-style on her head, walking quickly down the hallway toward her room. I was horrified! What if he had turned around? What if she had fallen down and made a scene? I confronted her later, and she said, "Mom, it's time for you to get these people out of our house!"

My next step was to buy a nicely decorated floor-to-ceiling screen and stretch it across the opening from the hallway to the living room. Problem solved.

One Friday evening, I was sitting with an important professional and his family, totally preoccupied with the family therapy I was conducting, when all of a sudden, I heard the screen fall to the floor, and my eighty-five-pound black Lab came rushing across the living room and into the lap of my client. I almost died! I made a decision that I had to get out of my home and find an office.

My dream was to find a sophisticated office on the sixteenth floor of an office building in Oak Brook. A friend who was a Realtor came to me and suggested I think about buying this little brown house in Wheaton. She said, "It's just like you." So I went to look at the house at 628 S. Prospect. It was small with one waiting room and three small rooms upstairs, a large downstairs room with carpeting, plus a kitchen. Outdoors, the place was overgrown with evergreen bushes and shrubs. I couldn't imagine what I would do with the entire house.

A good friend of mine, formerly a writer for United Airlines, got excited about the place. He started writing brochures for me. And he envisioned what we could do to make the outside presentable. There was a huge evergreen tree in the front yard, and I was hooked. *That would make a beautiful Christmas tree next year!* I thought. I bought the place, and we had an open house February 4, 1983, to celebrate the opening of our new office.

I had to sleuth a bit in order to find out where and how to get my Christmas tree decorated. I finally found a company in Hinsdale that would sell me the one thousand bulbs and bring their cherry picker equipment to decorate the tree for not too much money. It was a beautiful sight. Every year, we would receive telephone calls, especially from older residents of DuPage County, saying, "Your tree is the most beautiful and the biggest in DuPage County. Please don't ever stop putting it up." And so we didn't. When I finally sold the house and moved to a new office in Wheaton, I left the new owners the one thousand bulbs, and they in turn promised to decorate the tree each year. I have never seen the tree lit up since I left.

By now, the transition was complete. I learned that there was a name for what I loved to do: entrepreneur. I now had an identity, and it felt right. I loved what I was doing—working twelve- and fourteen-hour days and feeling full of energy. I knew this was what I was meant to do, and I would do it by God's grace for as long as I continued to be blessed with clients.

HANDLING THE PROBLEMS OF OUR TIMES*

Patricia Pape

The new offices of Pape & Associates in Wheaton offer services that reflect the problems of today: chemical dependency, employee assistance, women's groups, parenting, relationship enrichment, and divorce adjustment.

Pape's new offices at 628 Prospect are located in a former home with a comfortable atmosphere, easing any fears of those who are entering therapy for the first time. Patricia's warmth and upbeat personality show her enjoyment of helping others. She has extensive experience as a therapist, is an employee assistance counselor for Toyota Motor Sales, and a consultant for Lutheran Social Services in Downers Grove.

Ms. Pape developed the treatment program for and was director of the first freestanding alcoholism treatment center in DuPage County. She also designed and directed the Addictions Counselor Training Program for the College of DuPage.

Patricia tries to make her women's groups aware of their choices, to look at their options, in or out of the home. She encourages them to do whatever *they* choose to do: stay at home and raise their children or take steps to begin a career.

"I love what I do. It's exciting, and I feel I'm really helping people. If anyone had told me ten years ago, that I would own my own business, I would have laughed at them," says Pape.

*Revised from August 31, 1983, *Wheaton Leader* article written by Shelia Woods.

SUCCESS

I learned that success is the love of a good man, good as defined by my father. Now I guess I must add my mother.

I will never forget my mother's words to me when I brought her over to see my brand-new office I was opening. This was my first business—my very own. I was so excited. I had the one thing I had gotten from her, the picture of an Aurora countryside painted by her friend, hung over the couch in the waiting room. I brought her into the house I had purchased to use as an office, fully expecting her to be as excited as I was. She stood quietly. Slowly her eyes scanned the room. Then she looked at me with a sad look in her eyes and said, "Oh, honey, I am so sorry … " She paused.

"But, Mom," I said, "this is a dream come true."

"Oh, honey, I am just so sorry that you couldn't find a good man!"

She looked puzzled, and suddenly everything became clear. This had nothing to do with her loving or not loving me. She simply *didn't get it.* The only goal in her life—and therefore, by extension, in mine—was to "find a good man." I realized that this was what my marriages had always been about, looking for the happiness that *she* said came only from finding the right man and getting his love and approval. What I was now choosing, at age forty-two, was to take my own road, alone, and with no one else's approval. Would I make it? I didn't know. But I had to try.

That happened on Friday, December 3, 1982. I received a call the next day to go to the hospital immediately. My daughter and I hurried over there. By the time we got there, my mother lay peacefully in the hospital bed. She was already dead. Therefore, those words from the day before have lingered with me, as they were her last significant words to me.

WRITER AND HEDGE CLIPPER:
MAN OF MANY TALENTS

Tom Germuska was the man behind the scenes. Many an afternoon he trimmed the hedges at the soon-to-be-opened office for Pape & Associates. And this was after he had sat down and written the brochures for the new office. We had pictures of the staff, lists of services and groups, and directions on how to find us.

I met Tom at a Parents Without Partners group in Glenn Ellyn, and we became best of friends. I valued Tom's opinions. He was a writer for United Airlines, so that was an important skill. He had good ideas for marketing and public relations. And nothing was beneath him: weeding, hedge clipping, or cutting the grass.

Tom is still around—thirty years later—and we still respect and value each other. Tom has accompanied me to many of the International Council on Alcohol and Addictions Conferences, where I have presented on a variety of subjects related to alcoholism, women, and Adult Children of Alcoholics. We have seen Vienna and Venice, and Tom is always supportive.

Thanks, Tom, for all you have done.

PAPE & ASSOCIATES START-UP

On Halloween night of 1981, the person who walked out of The Abbey with me was Leighton Clark. We spent many hours sitting at my kitchen table, talking about how to start Pape & Associates. His skills at doing employee assistance programs complimented my clinical skills. We have remained close over the years, although we have taken different paths. The two of us share many treatment and life philosophies. We have participated in many of our major transitions and turning points with each other and rejoiced at each other's successes. He has been a major support in my life, both personally and professionally, and he is one of the people I am grateful to know.

DREAM COME TRUE*

When Pat Grover left Aurora, she never envisioned returning at all, much less as a business owner. Pat Grover Pape, now a psychotherapist, opened an office in a house at 581 Sullivan Road, Aurora. This was her new Aurora "home."

Pat had always wanted a family room with a fireplace. This is her dream come true. Pat offers individual, marital, family, and group psychotherapy. She's also developing employee assistance programs for area industry.

It's the story of how Pat returned to Aurora that intrigues many people. Pat had been a cheerleader at West Aurora High School until she graduated in 1958. She then went to Northwestern University in Evanston, where she majored in sociology and graduated in 1962.

Pat then headed for San Diego and a family of her own—her son, Scott, now a sophomore at Illinois Institute of Technology, and a daughter, Debbie, who is a freshman at Eastern Illinois University. When Pat returned to the Midwest in 1968, she and her family settled in Wheaton. Pat's roles became: mother, wife, PTA volunteer, Sunday school teacher, and Junior Women's Club member. She also worked six hours a day for $3 an hour as a church secretary.

Ten years ago, Pat and her husband divorced. A friend told her that she could do much more than the church office work, and that she was worth more than $3 an hour.

After Pat was divorced, she worked as a secretary for the DuPage County Diversionary Division, while simultaneously attending George Williams College for a master's degree in social work. "I worked full time, went to school full time, and was a full-time parent," she said. "My friends really encouraged me—you just can't do something like that without a good support system. I depended on my friends for help, too. As a mother, I had a lot of guilt about going back to school and work." Pat found that the kids did better in school when she was in school too. They all worked together.

Pape explains that she has a "high energy level." She firmly believes that a person "should play hard as well as work hard." That's why she took dance lessons at Fred Astaire Dance Studio two nights a week while she was working and going to graduate school. Pat said, "It was therapeutic. But my kids, Scott and Debbie, were always my top priority. Sunday was family day, and we always had dinner together. My hours were flexible enough so I could be there for them on special occasions if they let me know in advance. I went to their track meets and served as room mother for each of them."

Eventually, Pape became a therapist in the Diversionary Division for DuPage County. The program involved all elements in a young person's life before he or she went through the court system. "I love family therapy," Pat said. "There are so many kids in trouble today. I worked with the whole system, the school, the court, family, and health care." Pape became an advocate of short-term treatment. "Brief treatment can work effectively, involving all elements in a person's life," she said. "Why take two years to do what you can do in three months with follow-ups? In eleven months, none of our families went back to court. It was working."

Pat also "loves to start new things." She developed and directed the program and staffing for The Abbey, the first freestanding alcoholism treatment center in DuPage County, just after earning her master's degree. "That's when it was not yet admitted that there was an alcoholism problem in DuPage County," she says. When new management took The Abbey over in 1981, Pape opened a private practice in her home. Her client base grew so dramatically that she opened a Wheaton office in September 1982. Today Pape has four associates in that office.

The Wheaton office is busy and Pat knew that many of her clients came from Aurora, so she bought the former home on Sullivan Road to open an Aurora office. Pape prefers a house because she loves the homey atmosphere it projects. What used to be the living room is now a comfortable waiting room. The former family room will be used for group sessions. Bedrooms have been turned into offices, and Pat hopes to turn the basement into a children's play area.

She expects that the greatest number of clients in family therapy and counseling will be struggling with alcoholism and chemical dependency. Because Pat continues to like something new, she personally is developing employee assistance programs (EAPs) for area industry. "An EAP is a confidential service that assists employees and their families to identify and resolve problems that affect job performance," Pat says. She assesses an employee's problem and refers him or her to an appropriate resource for help. In an EAP, she would not refer clients to her own office.

A key problem for industry today is chemical dependency. Estimates are that 10 percent of the workforce is using alcohol at a level that affects job performance. The idea of EAPs came to light in the 1970s.

"Today about 50 percent of the Fortune 500 companies have an EAP," Pape says, "and I want to offer the same chance to companies in and around Aurora." Pape already provides EAP services to Caterpillar Tractor Co. and the FAA operation in Aurora. Cynthia Strump, a social worker formerly with the Mercy Center for Health Care Adolescent Unit, has become one of Pape's associates in the Aurora office.

*Revised from August 31, 1984, *Beacon News* article written by Cathy Cryer.

WOMEN OF ACHIEVEMENT AWARD, ENTREPRENEURIAL CATEGORY*

In 1986, Women in Management, Oak Brook, Illinois, selected Patricia A. Pape, clinical psychotherapist, whose business offers individual, couple, family and group psychotherapy services as well as comprehensive employee assistance programs, to receive the Women of Achievement Award, Entrepreneurial Category. Prior to starting her own private practice in 1981, she was with the DuPage County Probation Department. She is a member of the Academy of Certified Social Workers and a Senior Certified Addictions Counselor.

When asked why she decided to go into private practice, Pat's answer was relatively simple: "Frankly, I've always been an entrepreneur, even when I was working for someone else. In my entire career, I've always been the person looking for the new ways, and the new concepts to develop. That's the true mark of an entrepreneur.

"I absolutely love starting new ventures. To me, entrepreneurship is that challenge—the fun of taking a concept from your mind and turning it into a reality."

She has two basic rules of advice for new or potential entrepreneurs:

1) Learn to live with confusion until your idea gels. Don't be afraid of this growth process; you'll live through the changes.

2) Have a support group. "The women support groups I belonged to made what I've done possible because they could see the potential in me and gave me the contacts and support necessary to accomplish those challenges."

In less than 10 years, Pat Pape's business has grown to four offices, with the addition of a Hinsdale location just this year, and offers the services of 17 counselors. Her other locations are in Wheaton, Schaumburg and Aurora.

*Revised from the *Women in Management, Inc., Newsletter,* Oak Brook chapter.

THE PAPE PARADIGM*

In 1987, at the International Council on Alcohol and Addictions, in Lausanne, Switzerland, Patricia A. Pape, president of Pape & Associates, gave her presentation of "Superwoman in the Workplace." She stressed planning a course of action, believing in yourself, praying a lot when things go wrong, and reexamining your actions. Only ten years earlier, Patricia was struggling economically as a $3.00 an hour church secretary. The leap from struggling housewife to being internationally recognized as a psychotherapist, speaker, and consultant did not happen overnight. She first had to do a lot of serious soul-searching.

She sat down and did a frank "self-inventory." On the positive side was placed her bachelors in Sociology. Then on the negative side, Pape was in her early 30s, divorced, and nearly broke. Pape realized that there were three objectives that were paramount in achieving her self-recognized career goals: 1) to be accepted by a graduate program and obtain a master's degree in social work; 2) to be accepted into a college that would help her fund her studies; and 3) to find a higher paying job with health benefits. Patricia, being one who never does anything in half measures, attacked all three problems at once.

Pape applied for a secretarial job with DuPage County Diversionary Division with the hope that this would not only be interesting, but would be advantageous to her career plans. She then applied to every school in the area. George Williams College took a chance on her and helped her get the funding for a graduate program. Patricia graduated a straight-A honors student in 1979. "Pure energy and luck" is the way she attributes her abilities to manage school, parenting and working full time. "I had extremely cooperative kids; they did better in school when I was in school too. They recognized the hope of a better future and worked right along with me."

Pape would start her day at 5 a.m. and still does. This "quiet time" provides an opportunity to organize and plan her day.

After graduation, Patricia became a licensed clinical social worker and certified addictions counselor. Opportunity came knocking when a counselor at the DuPage County Diversionary Division quit with little notice. She moved from the typewriter to the counseling office, looking forward to newfound challenges, as did her clients. The success rate in the probation department can be measured by how often families are back in court within a 12-month period. The normal rate of success with non-returns is between 30–45 percent; Patricia's was 100 percent. She was honored with an award and was asked to teach a Task-Centered Casework course on how this was accomplished. Pape is a believer in short-term treatment, asking, "Why take two years to do what can be done in three months with follow-ups?"

During this time Pape found she possessed an entrepreneurial spirit — that pronounced ability to develop ideas. She then moved on to developing programs and staffing at The Abbey, the first freestanding alcoholism treatment center in DuPage County. Before The Abbey opened in 1980, no one would acknowledge a problem with alcohol in the county. In 1981, a new conglomerate in the health care field took over The Abbey. Patricia went from a salary of $30,000 a year to zero.

"I did what everyone else does — picked myself up and went to the nearest unemployment office, where I stood in line with some of the same people I had treated the week before." Pape looked for answers by using the same positive/negative system of self-appraisal that had worked so well for her before.

Patricia liked being her own boss so much that she decided to start a private practice out of her own home. By word of mouth, her counseling practice grew dramatically, as did a new set of problems. Neighbors were not happy with the parking problems; juggling clients, children, and a dog in a residential office was getting to be too complicated. When her 120-pound dog, Duchess, jumped into the lap of one of her clients, Pape knew that she had to find a commercial office space. Patricia knew that her patients were more receptive and open in a home-type atmosphere. She talked a loan officer at a local bank into lending her enough money to purchase another home to convert into offices. Pape expanded her practice into two of the state's fastest-growing suburbs — Aurora and Schaumburg. Pape & Associates grew to include eight associates, two interns and three support staff.

At the same time, Patricia wrote a training program for alcoholism and addictions counselors at the College of DuPage, the first such program in the State of Illinois, and became its first director.

Pape feels she constantly needs "new world to conquer." She became an innovator in the development of employee assistance programs (EAPs). Patricia estimates that 10 percent of the workforce is using alcohol or other substances at a level that affects job performance. The Federal Aviation Association Operations in Aurora, the Motorola

Corporation in Schaumburg, and the Northbrook School District in Glenview have used her services.

Pape's latest undertaking is launching the Illinois Chapter of the Children of Adult Alcoholics (ICCOA), of which she is vice chairperson. She's constantly on the go, traveling the county on countless speaking engagements, on the topic of chemical dependency. Patricia gives the following advice to anyone thinking of embarking upon a new life: "Plan a course of action, keep believing in yourself, and pray a lot. When things go wrong and doors seem to be closing, reexamine your options; it may be another door opening the way to something wonderful."

*Revised from *Management Digest* article written by Candy R. Lee.

COLLEGE OF DUPAGE ADADE WHEELER AWARD
NATIONAL WOMEN'S HISTORY MONTH 1998

Nominee:

Patricia A. Pape
Pape & Associates
618 S. West St.
Wheaton, IL 60187
630-668-8710

Nominated by:

Thomas A. Germuska
1335 Westbury Drive
Hoffman Estates, IL 60195
847-934-1984

Nominated for the Adade Wheeler Award, is Patricia A. Pape, in recognition of her tireless efforts to enhance the lives of women. Patricia demonstrates daily this advocacy in both her personal and professional life.

The foundation of her compassion for women's issues was buttressed by her own struggle to return to college for graduate studies as a single mother in the 1970s. Patricia's career as a psychotherapist has furthered her mission to empower women (before the term became popular), as has her steadfast endorsement of separate treatment of women for alcoholism and substance abuse.

Patricia opened a private practice in Wheaton in 1981. Since then her business has grown significantly. Today, she has a dozen associates and five interns (more than two-thirds are women) who provide individual, couple, family and group psychotherapy to clients at offices in Aurora, Hinsdale, and Schaumburg as well as Wheaton.

She also consults with both public and private organizations on the design, implementation and monitoring of comprehensive employee assistance programs. That Patricia advocates on behalf of women is evident in the way she operates her business. Her associates enjoy flexible scheduling to easily integrate their work and family lives. Clients needing childcare accommodations can get services without worrying about a babysitter. Weekly therapy groups address a variety of women's issues, and no woman has ever been denied help because of financial hardship.

As a consequence of Ms.Pape's own success, she is often sought out by others for advice and counsel regarding the establishment of their own businesses. She has been able to help other women advance their careers. Not a week goes by that she doesn't spend an hour or more mentoring other women with respect to entrepreneurial issues or answering inquiries from students.

Dozens of these students, more than 50 of them women, have gone on to serve internships under Pat's supervision. Some have come from the College of DuPage Addictions Counselor Training Program. Patricia designed the program in 1979 and taught it for nine years.

Other students are master's level graduate students from area colleges and universities.

During Ms. Pape's career, she has been a proponent of distinct treatment programs for women with alcohol and substance abuse problems. She started the first women's sobriety groups in DuPage County in 1981 and thereafter championed the cause of specialized treatment in national and international professional organization.

> *She organized the first conference on "Women's Issues in Chemical Dependency" (1986) for the national Alcohol and Drug Problems Association and continued to shepherd that activity until 1995.

> *From 1987 through 1992, she was a presenter at the annual conference of the International Congress on Alcohol and Addictions on the subject of women's issues in employee assistance programs.

> *She served on the Women's issues committee of the Employee Assistance Professional Association for five years.

In addition to her personal appearances, Ms. Pape is the author of nine articles, one pamphlet, and chapters in two books on issues related to the treatment of alcoholism and substance abuse in women.

Her strong voice to educate others about critical issues for women, this time on the subject of domestic violence, was heard in October 1997, when she organized a monthlong Domestic Violence Awareness program at her church (St. Paul Lutheran in Wheaton) and published an article, "Shedding Light on Domestic Violence," in *Metropolitan Chicago Life*, a monthly newspaper distributed by the Metropolitan Chicago Synod of the Evangelical Lutheran Church in America.

Ms. Pape's actions to encourage personal growth in women are superbly illustrated by the Women's Weekend Empowerment

Workshops presented between 1992 and 1996 at the Cenacle Retreat House in Warrenville. She designed, developed and wrote workshop materials and presented these experiential retreats, which enabled women to increase self-esteem, become more assertive, identify and express anger, and learn how to create healthy relationships.

She is also the designer and coleader of a 12-week workshop in which women at her church have been able to explore their spirituality. Participants in the series were able to redefine their images of God as well as explore their connections to God, to other women and to men.

Although many women look to Pat Pape as a role model, the most important one is her daughter, Debra Pape Skjerven. Not only has Debbie followed in her mother's footsteps as a therapist, the two teamed up to present daylong mother-daughter workshops at the Cenacle on Mother's Day in 1994–1996. Together they helped mothers and daughters enhance their relationships with each other as women.

There is no one more deserving of the Adade Wheeler Award than my friend Pat Pape.

FOX RIVER VALLEY DISTRICT AWARDS DINNER

1998 SOCIAL WORKER OF THE YEAR

PAT PAPE

Pat developed and directed the first freestanding alcoholism treatment center in DuPage County. In addition, Pat developed the curriculum for, and directed, the Addictions Counselor Training Program for the College of DuPage. In 1981, Pat founded *Pape & Associates* to provide clinical services and employee assistance programs for businesses and educational institutions. Pat has been an assisting minister at St. Paul Lutheran Church in Wheaton for the past five years. Her latest project involves developing an Intergenerational Village, including teens from Sunny Ridge in Wheaton and senior citizens.

Congratulations, Pat!

A SURROGATE FATHER

Barry Weber was my consulting psychologist. We met every few weeks to talk about my work with clients. Our relationship started long ago, the first year that I was in business. I knew his mother, so I wrote to him of that relationship and asked if he would work with me. Over the years, we had agreed to disagree about our theories on alcoholism and addictions. I attempted to take what was helpful and leave the rest.

Eventually, we began to focus more and more on our relationship and also on personal issues. Barry knew my personal history: dysfunctional family, two alcoholic parents, and abuse issues. He never judged and never preached.

I remember the day we talked about my anxiety regarding my upcoming presentation in Vienna. I had become so fearful of making a mistake or forgetting what I was going to say. And, of course, I knew intellectually that I could literally scare myself with my own negative or critical thoughts.

"Just imagine I am standing there, right next to you on the stage. And if you feel frightened, I will simply hold you up," Barry said.

"What if I faint?" I continued along the path of fearful thoughts.

"I will simply bring you a glass of water," Barry replied softly.

"At what point are you going to stop being kind and start judging me?" I asked.

"Not at all," Barry said.

And so we went back and forth: me trying to figure out something I could do to cause him to become critical or shaming of me, and him simply refuting that possibility. I realize now that it was still hard for me to trust a man and hard to accept compliments.

I went to Vienna, made the flight with no problems, gave my presentation successfully, and returned home. I have often thought about how wonderful it felt to have such acceptance. It was almost as if there was nothing I could do to get him to not accept me.

Several years after that interaction, we had an open house to celebrate twenty years in business. Barry came to congratulate me and my staff. I still have a picture that was taken that day. Barry had auburn hair, sparkling blue eyes, and full lips that tended to turn up often into a smile. He was standing next to me, about six inches taller than I am, arm around my shoulder, smiling. I felt safe and approved of, and I appreciated his going out of his way to be there.

I never saw him again. Not too long after our open house, Barry suffered a heart attack during one of his men's therapy groups.

Someone revived him once, but the second time he didn't come back. Today, I am even more grateful for my memories and that picture.

I realize with hindsight that this man was the father I never had. I think that his kindness and acceptance helped me to be able to accept myself. The healing of old wounds is a slow process, but eventually this has also helped me to heal old wounds with my father. I am better able to understand his woundedness and pain. Today, I can forgive both my father and myself. Much of this is a result of knowing Barry Weber, my surrogate father, who taught me much about self-acceptance.

PAPE & ASSOCIATES
OFFICE LOCATIONS

Friday, February 4, 1983
>   Open House – 628 S. Prospect, Wheaton, IL 60187

Friday, September 21, 1984
>   Open House – 581 Sullivan Road, Aurora, IL 60506

September 1985
>   2050 E. Algonquin Road, Suite 605, Schaumburg, IL 60195

November 1988
>   Professional Counseling Services, 522 West Chestnut, Suite 1D, Hinsdale, IL 60521

Friday, September 29, 1989
>   618 S. West Street, Wheaton, IL 60187

Friday, September 29, 1989
>   2040 Algonquin Road, Suite 504, Schaumburg, IL 60195

September 1994
>   1325 Remington Road, Suite J, Schaumburg, IL 60173

Friday, November 2, 2001
>   Twentieth anniversary

Friday, November 3, 2006
>   Twenty-fifth anniversary

SPIRITUAL JOURNEY

THE PHOENIX RISES AGAIN

It was Pat Lee, my sponsor, mentor and friend, who, in 1983, taught me the ancient story of the Phoenix. We were sitting in her kitchen, having a cup of coffee, with the rays of sunshine streaming in the window, when she said, "I think it's significant you're driving a Pontiac Phoenix; it's sort of symbolic of the story of your life." I sat there, saying nothing, having no idea what she was talking about. Since she was one of those wise women and mentors, I trusted she would explain.

Several times in your life," she said, you have felt as if you had lost everything, as if you were dead. This reminds me of the Phoenix, the bird who rose out of its own ashes and was able to fly again. And now, this is the make and model of your car. Do you see this as a metaphor of your life?"

I could. And I have never forgotten that day or the message. Several times since then, I have lost important people in my life. One time, I lost almost everything financially. Remembering and visualizing the Phoenix rising has given me the courage to bounce back, to take risks, and to try new things.

I believe that until you learn to say good-bye, you cannot say hello. Letting go of the past is essential to living in the present. All endings are new beginnings. Life progresses in cycles, and the death of winter always brings the new life of spring. Out of our deepest losses, we often gain our greatest insights, and our empathy for others grows. The Chinese symbol for "danger" is twofold: "crisis" and "opportunity."

All of this brings me to the present—starting my two-year journey to learn how to write and, hopefully, to publish a book for women that will bring healing and transformation. I am willing to take this risk. Otherwise, I will never know if I could have done it. I tell all women with whom I work to dream big. And I will not do any less for myself.

Even though I no longer have my Phoenix, my Phoenix is within. As I steer along the highway, I look up at the sky and smile, thinking, *Let the journey begin.*

KEEP FOLLOWING THE STAR

I can still hear her voice: "Keep following the star." She gave me a Christmas card just before she died, with the three wise men on the front and those words written on the inside. One of the wise men looks like a woman to me. This reminds me of her: she was so wise.

Pat Lee was a surrogate mother to me: strong but loving, kind and gentle. She encouraged me during a difficult transition time in my life. I had just gotten divorced and started my life as a single parent of two children, ages five and seven. It was 1986 when she gave me that card. I still have it, along with the journal. I have never been one to journal in the past, but now that I have taken journaling and writing classes, I am more open to completing the task.

What was it about Pat that was so impressive? It wasn't her looks, which were quite plain, her light brown hair gently pulled back into a soft bun in the back of her head. Her brown eyes appeared so deep and transparent, I could almost see through them. I can still hear her raspy, low voice softly telling me, "You can do it!" And even today I think of her when I need a confidence boost.

I have never met someone so nonjudgmental and accepting, no matter what my actions were. I remember once telling her something awful that I had done. She just looked at me with those brown eyes, filled with love, and said, "And? I'm not supposed to love you anymore?"

I responded in disbelief, "There seems to be nothing I can do to get you to stop loving me!"

She responded, "Hey, you're getting it." Truly, I have never in my life had such an experience.

Once, when I had complicated my life in such a way that I was totally overwhelmed, she looked at me, smiled, and said, "If there is a hard way of doing something, and an easy way, you will always pick the hard way. Instead of just walking in the front door of the house, you walk all the way around to the back door, via the vacant lot next door." No judgment, just stating an accurate observation. I have never forgotten that either.

Pat was one of the most influential women in my life. I carry her in my head, where I still hear her saying, "Keep following the star." I have followed her instructions, all these twenty-five years, and what an exciting journey it has been. "Thank you, Pat."

PELICANS

Many years ago, I was leading a retreat at the Warrenville Cenacle with Sister Patsy Pafco. She was doing a guided meditation for the early Saturday morning service. I don't remember the subject, but I will never forget the image of the pelican that kept coming into my imagination.

I was telling her about it after the service, totally discounting and making a joke about seeing a pelican. She stopped me and asked if I had any idea of the symbolism behind the pelican. I answered, "No, I don't."

She told me the moving story of the pelican. After the father pelican murdered his young, the mother pelican revived her children by sprinkling on them her blood from her own breast. She became the symbol of Christ and of the female image of God.

How meaningful that was for me! I have always struggled with the church's masculine images of God. And here came God, into my own experience on the retreat, to be the feminine for me. How comforting.

Again, in answer to the ongoing question "And where is God in all this?" the answer is "Right there beside me and within me!" Thank you, God, for another of your undeserved gifts of grace.

A COINCIDENCE OR A MIRACLE?

It had been two days. I still had the pain in my lower right side. I could hardly walk, and it was getting worse. "It'll go away soon," I reassured myself. I was not the type to run to doctors at the first sign of a problem. "I can handle it myself." I learned those words well from my father, who used to say to me, "If you want it done right, do it yourself." And I did.

By midmorning the next day, I decided I couldn't do my training workout. That should have been my first clue since I never missed one. I called my nurse friend Mary. She said, "This has gone on too long. We're going to the ER." And off we went.

"Your appendix is fine," said the doctor, "but we picked up a good-sized mass in your left lung. We think it's cancer." His voice was cold, his manner matter-of-fact.

"Okay," I said, remaining cool. "Now what do I do?" I held it together while talking to him. Shortly after, he walked out of the room, on to his next patient. And that's when, totally out of my control, my body suddenly started shaking.

On September 1, 2002, I had been scared into quitting smoking when an error by the X-ray technician caused me to think there might be a tumor in my lungs. Now there was one.

Denial and adrenaline carried me through the next seven days of procedures and tests. I was supported by my church community's love and prayers through the surgery and recovery. Three years later, I am still cancer free. By the way, we never did figure out what caused the pain in my right side. Or maybe I should say who.

FAITH THE SIZE OF A MUSTARD SEED

"If you have faith the size of a mustard seed, you can move mountains," Jesus said. I have a pin with a small clear container on it and in the container are many mustard seeds, about the size of the head of a pin. So I always think of them and wonder why I am not moving mountains.

Perhaps my definition of mountains is not accurate. I might have moved a mountain when I got through my divorce, or when I started my own business, or when I survived after one of my employees took half of my clients. Was that having faith? And if so, how do I define faith?

Several weeks ago, I was feeling pretty discouraged, so I wrote in my journal. I asked myself, "Where is my faith?" When I took this question to my spiritual director, she said, "Uh, you're here." Boy, that was pretty disappointing. I guess I thought that if I had faith it would mean a Moses-type experience on the mountaintop with God, and that has never happened to me. So for me faith has meant simply learning to live in the now, put one foot in front of the other, and do the next right thing as. Pretty ordinary, huh? Perhaps the ordinary is sacred after all.

DEAR GOD

Dear God,

The year is ending at midnight tonight, and I decided I needed to write you a letter. I am disappointed in my attempts this year to get to know you. As I say that, my throat constricts, and I feel tears welling up in my eyes. Why is that? I started to say, "God forbid I be upset with *you* for your attempts, because you are perfect." But I also don't think you forbid me to be upset with you.

My last request in this year is to show yourself in such a way that I am not afraid to die, that I will have such faith in you, that I will trust you to be on the other side to greet me.

Okay, the road to Emmaeus. You are walking with two of your disciples. One of my favorite stories. They don't know who you are. May I walk with you? Instead of Emmaeus, could we walk down the Prairie Path? Who are you, Jesus? I can feel my insides longing for you, longing to know you. So why do I keep saying I don't know you? I have struggled with the idea of a God who requires a specific belief system in order for us to "go to heaven." I also struggle with a God who requires nothing of us. Where are you on that continuum?

My spiritual director says we complicate things too much, that each of us is a gift of love from God to the world. And maybe not the *whole* world, but just the five feet of space that surrounds me. She tells me that you are a relational God, and what you most desire is a relationship with me. *That* is hard for me to understand. But last week when she said, "God is right here in this room," I said "It's hard not to believe what you just said." So I guess I took it on faith.

I talk about being a *conduit* for you. I want to have whatever words and actions you would have me say or do simply go through me. Sometimes I can feel that, and when I do, it is like someone pouring warm water through a hole in my head, down through my whole body. Such a wonderful feeling. But there are other times when I can't find you and have absolutely no idea what you want me to do.

My prayer life is so dry! I rarely talk to you, and I am forever forgetting to pray for the people I say I am going to. If I do, I just visualize them and figure that you know what they need. I also figure you know what I need, so I rarely ask for specific things. I read somewhere that my longings are your grace. Enough grace! I really want to see you and know you, but I also don't want to die yet.

I am stuck, aren't I? I am thinking that the last sentence is sort of an either/or proposition. If I want to see you perfectly (not "through a glass darkly"), then I will

be on the other side of the veil. So I think of what someone said: "I'd rather believe in God and find out there is no God than to not believe in you and find out you are real."

SPIRITUALITY

Ever since I was a little girl, I have been obsessed with doing and being enough and with getting it right. And here I was, nearly seventy years later, when my spiritual director asked, "How was your Christmas?" I responded, "I don't feel like I did enough, felt enough, or thought enough about God. Like, it's *God's* birthday, not mine, but you'd think I was in charge of God's birthday party!"

I also told her I am going to attempt to describe my "spiritual journey" now, and I feel totally overwhelmed. Somehow I guess I thought I would be further along after seeking and searching all these years. I feel out of control when I have so many more questions than answers. Oh, I know, Rilke would say to live the questions, but if I am totally honest, I don't even know what that means.

As I thought about my childhood and religion, I realized I'd spent a lot of time trying to figure our what my *earthly* father wanted and trying to please him. Perhaps this set the pattern for my adult religious behavior. I remember Father's Day when I was four or five years old, sitting in my closet the night before—door closed so if he came into my bedroom, he would not see that the light was on—and desperately trying to write a perfect poem that would make my father understand how much I loved him ... and how much I wanted to do what he said and to make him happy. I can remember the feeling in my stomach, a bit of anxiety and a bit of longing and sadness and disconnection, because I didn't know for sure if I was getting it right. The next day I would make pancakes, and my little brother and I would give Dad breakfast in bed.

As I look back on it now, on Sunday mornings, when I would sit on my father's lap and he would read me *The Teenie Weenies*, that was about as close as I remember feeling the way God's love would feel for me. (I wonder if God reads *The Teenie Weenies*. I sure love it when my spiritual director reads a story to me. God must speak to me directly through her.)

When I was a child, we joined New England Congregational Church on Galena Boulevard in Aurora. Somehow I always had the impression that belonging to this church was a status symbol, more about us than about God. The West Aurora High School a cappella choir always sang on Christmas Eve. I was in the choir, and my parents were so proud of me. All the important people in town belonged to this church.

The only real memory I have of Sunday School at that church was probably when I was about ten, looking at Jesus hanging on the cross, with only a white cloth covering his genitals. Some of us girls got to talking about his body and what he must look like without the white cloth. Then we all felt really sinful! How in the world could we be saying things like that about God's own body? We all knew God was supposed to be Spirit, not body. This is an issue I have struggled with all my life. It is probably one of the reason's I always loved *Jesus Christ Superstar* and Mary Magdalene's love song for Jesus. The only difference is that today I can say that I find Jesus to be attractive and not feel it is sinful.

When I was a junior in high school, I got connected to Young Life out of Wheaton College. My best friend Judy Brauer had the Young Life meetings at her home, and Jan Spring and Bill Starr led the group. How uplifting it felt to sing the songs and hear the message. Then I went to Frontier Ranch in Buena Vista, Colorado. Each night, someone would give a talk about turning your life over to Christ and invite people to come down to the campfire and do so. I would have done it, but I wasn't sure if I knew how to do it right, and I sure didn't want to screw this up because it had to do with being with God for eternity versus going to hell for eternity. What pressure I felt. When I finally stood up and did it, I have no recollection of what I said. But I will never forget what my counselor said: "Pat, I have never seen anyone struggle so hard or cry so much when accepting Christ." She didn't know that I was trying to get it *perfect*.

I had a special rock that I sat on every morning to read my Bible and talk to God. I watched the sun come up behind the clouds—one time I took a picture that truly looked like the clouds with a silver lining behind them. All the time I was there, I had this sense that God was just on the other side of the clouds, just out of my reach, and that I needed to keep being more and reaching farther out to some mysterious place.

In college, I spent a lot of time on the chapel board and also the Young Life Leadership group. This was where I met Dave. I fell in love with him and took him home to my parents. They kept calling him by the wrong name (the name of my first husband), and my father told me that I should marry my first husband, not Dave, because he would be more "successful." My mother agreed (she never did anything else). And, of course, I went along with it all because in the sixties I never had my own opinion or my own voice. I realize now that one of the things I was looking for was someone with the same spiritual value system I had.

In my senior year in college, I became engaged to my first husband. His mother took me aside and told me in very clear terms that there were two problems that were going to interfere with me marrying her son: (1) I wasn't Lutheran; and (2) I was going to be "fat and dumpy in my middle-age years." So I lost the twenty pounds I had gained my freshman year, and I volunteered to become Lutheran. And we got married three days after graduation from college. Today, I am still Lutheran and really have grown to love the religion.

During the sixties, I certainly wandered from God—there was lots of drinking and other mood-altering substances—yet even during this decade, I always had a sense of seeking and searching and longing to connect, but not feeling pure enough. In my work today with women and alcoholism and spirituality, I have done a lot of reading of Carl Jung. He believes that much of using alcohol as an escape and a medication for physical and emotional and spiritual pain is related to the meaning of the Latin word for alcohol, *spiritus.* He pointed out that we use the same word for the spiritual thirst of our being for wholeness, the union with God, as we do the craving for alcohol. His formula was: *spiritus contra spiritum.*

When I walked away from my marriage in 1972, I was alone, yet not alone. I discovered I had to do the next right thing, and somehow I just "knew" what that was. I used all the tools I had: therapy, 12-step programs, supportive friends, reading, and attempting to pray. I say "attempting" because this is something I have spent forty years trying to learn. I tried kneeling down by my bed; I tried meditating every morning and clearing my mind; I tried journaling; I tried praying for knowledge of God's will—only to get into games like "If it rains, then that means … " and then "If the sun shines, then that means … " I read books on discernment, only to become more confused. I felt totally discouraged at times: the more I tried, the worse I felt! What was I doing wrong?

There were days where I felt like I was on a desert, crawling in the scorching sun in the sand, heading for something, but I didn't know what. My heart felt empty, and I was filled with despair. The longing was a physical feeling by then. Twice I thought I had found God's will for my life in yet another marriage. And that wasn't it. Each time I would "start over," I would be filled with anticipation: "This time I got it right!" Only it wasn't. And I thought I couldn't bear another disappointment.

In the 1990s, one of the members of the worship and music board at our church asked me if I would work on an Inclusive Language Project with him. I said yes, having absolutely no idea what I was getting into. This ended up being a turning point in my life. I read books on the women of the Bible. I studied Sophia (Wisdom) tradition of the feminine face of God. We stopped calling God "He" and didn't use any pronouns at all. Much of the ELCA has changed to Inclusive Language. The first time I was assisting minister and wrote the prayers to God, our Mother and our Father, I actually told two of my friends to pray for me that God would not come down and strike me with lightening. God did not, and I have been praying to God our Mother and Father ever since. What a gentle feeling I get, a warmth throughout my body, a feeling of acceptance for looking like God the Mother. I changed a lot during those two years.

MY JOURNEY INTO BAPTISM AND BEYOND

The seeds were planted several years ago, although I had no idea then, when a dear friend who is a genealogist began to work with me on putting together all of the pieces of my family heritage.

Then I signed up for Pastor Steve Meysing's six-week study class of the Augsburg Confession (I have since learned to expect the unexpected when I sign up for his classes). I wasn't raised Lutheran, had never been through confirmation, and I wanted to learn about my Lutheran heritage since I had been a member of St. Paul Lutheran Church for over twenty-five years. We kept talking about the importance of our baptismal covenant, and I decided to get a copy of my baptismal certificate from the congregational church of my childhood. I found out that, due to a natural disaster, all records from 1938–1943 had been totally destroyed. Now I would never be able to know for sure if I had been baptized. I was pretty sure I had been, since my brother's infant baptism papers from 1943 were there.

I finally went to our senior pastor Melody Eastman and told her of my quandary. She told me there was a service of baptism/reaffirmation of baptism (conditional baptism) that functioned as a baptism if that had never been done, or as a reaffirmation of baptism if baptism had been done. She was willing, under the circumstances, to do a private service in our chapel, after our regular services. We set the date for Sunday, August 13, 2000, since my daughter and her family would be in town that weekend to give a sixtieth birthday celebration for me the night before. Little did I know what a powerful experience the next few months would be for me.

I found myself sitting in our pre-baptismal meeting full of anxiety and trepidation, which totally surprised me. I decided it was a great deal easier to be baptized as an infant, having your parents and sponsors answer all the questions for you. Instead, here I sat as an adult, having struggled through "crises of faith" and having been well acquainted with doubts. I had two strong reactions. The first was a compelling need to talk about everything in my life that I felt unworthy about. I found a couple of old unhealed wounds surfacing, and I experienced a great deal of emotional pain that completely caught me off guard. Second, all my past faith crises resurfaced. I have struggled in the last decade with reconciling the reality of the male images and language of the Bible and the church with my need for female images and language to describe God. I expressed my fears of not being able to honestly answer yes to the questions in the baptismal service, and I refused to be dishonest in my answers.

Meanwhile, Pastor Eastman simply listened nonjudgmentally and compassionately, with acceptance, and suggested saying, "I want to believe" or "With God's help, I believe." There was simply nothing I could offer up that could "disqualify" me from being baptized. She ended our meeting with a prayer to "Our Mother God," asking for healing and for acceptance of all of the blessings and love God wants to give us. This was to become a theme for me—*receiving* God's love, forgiveness, and presence in my life as opposed to *doing* it myself. In fact, I couldn't believe it when I heard myself say, half jokingly, as I stood up to leave, "You mean I *qualified*? Me, who professes a faith in God's grace, not based on my merit. Where did this come from? Did I think this was a club I had to be voted into?"

Meanwhile, a few days before my baptism, I received some painful news. My son and his wife, who also live in Wheaton, refused to attend the service. So my three granddaughters, ages four, eight, and ten would not be there. I was devastated and called Pastor Eastman for support. I remember being angry with God and asking, "Is this God's idea of a bad joke?" (Why do we always blame *God* when something does not go as *we* plan for it to go?) I still remember her answer: "You can only heal yourself; you cannot heal your son."

At about 7:00 on Sunday morning of my baptism, I was at the Dumpster by my office, a block from the church, dressed in an old pair of sweats. I was getting rid of some trash from my birthday party the night before. Suddenly, I heard a voice calling, "Pat, Pat!" I remember looking up toward the sky—did I think it was God calling? I realized it was the senior pastor, in her car on the street behind me. "Pat, I'll see you later." She later laughed and said she enjoyed watching me looking up into the sky, almost as if I expected to see Christ returning. I do believe that my sense of God's closeness was so strong that day that nothing would have surprised me.

The baptismal service was powerful and memorable. The pastor brought a beautiful crystal bowl to hold the water, putting it on a simple stand. Later, my two-year-old grandson Matthew was exploring, and we heard him say "wa-wa" as he dumped the entire pitcher of water onto the chapel carpet. As we ran to get towels and the pastor was down mopping up the carpet, I thought of Jesus saying, "Suffer the little children."

The service was one I have heard and participated in many times, with two key exceptions. First, when I heard the words "I believe in God our Mother and Father ... " I was extremely touched and found myself without any hesitation being able to profess my faith in God, Jesus Christ, and the Holy Spirit.

Second, I remember asking how much water the pastor was planning to pour on my head. I had only seen one adult baptism, and it was done with a small shell, only on the person's forehead. She said, "As much as I can!" As I felt the water trickling through my hair and running down my face when I lifted my head, I remember a part of me wishing I hadn't used hair spray that day. But I remember the rest of me feeling such a sense of joy and strong presence of God that I didn't care.

My friend Dorothy, who had been helping me with the genealogy, and her husband, George, were my baptismal sponsors. It is an interesting experience as an adult to ask two other adults to be your baptismal sponsors. But it was extremely special. And the friends who attended the service added to the specialness of the day.

The day after my baptism, I received the news from my doctor's office that he thought I might have cancer. I would need further tests and some outpatient surgery. Again, I called the senior pastor and said, "Is this some kind of a test?" I requested her prayers. And I was pretty scared. All of which didn't seem to fit with the "faith" I had just professed the day before.

A few weeks later, when this was all over and the outcome was positive, I stopped by Pastor Eastman's office to let her know the good news. I remember saying, "I am so grateful; God still has something left for me to do." And I will never forget her quiet response: "Or to receive." There was that theme again: stop trying to *do* it all. Relax, rest, and *allow* God to love you and to give you the grace that is freely offered.

The week after that, I got the results of my bone density test and was diagnosed with osteopenia—me, who never gets sick and who feels wonderful and energetic most all the time. This has led to a series of lifestyle changes as well as an increased awareness of my own mortality and the fragility of our earthly bodies. But I didn't really feel like dealing with yet a third test.

A month after my baptism, I began a nine-week spiritual formation class that Pastor Meysing was offering. We studied six of the classic Christian spirituality traditions. At one point, I was reading about Jesus's baptism and how "immediately following his baptism, the Holy Spirit led him out into the desert to be tempted three times by Satan." Suddenly, a light bulb went on in my head, and I remembered seeing an analogy between Jesus's three temptations and my three "tests." I certainly knew what it was like to feel as if I were on a desert, searching and longing for God's presence. But, then, so did Jesus. Was I to be above being tested? Or was this God's way of saying to me, "No matter what happens, I am with you, and that is all you need." I have no idea what the final outcomes of these three tests will be. But I do *know,* beyond a shadow of a doubt, that God is with and within me, and this knowledge fills me with a joy and peace such as I have never known.

GOOD FRIDAY SERVICE

It was a night service on Good Friday. The church was dark. People filed in silently and sat down. The seven candles on the altar would be extinguished as we remembered Jesus's last words from the cross. I have been coming to this service almost every year, since I joined the church forty-five years ago when I was twenty-five, a single mom with two children. I always wear black, and I am usually sobered by this particular service.

Soft music played in the background. Approximately 150 people filled the pews. After the service, when the church was completely dark, our tall young associate pastor dragged a roughly cut six-and-a-half-foot wooden cross slowly down the center aisle. The wood was pine, saved from our last live Christmas tree. There was something engaging about his long, slow journey to the altar. After he laid the cross against the altar, we were invited to gather around the cross and contemplate the crucifixion. People were silently gathering. I had never done this before, and my stomach twittered a bit. I was anxious because it was a new experience, and there were probably forty people who would be watching me down by the cross. In all my lifetime of being a Christian—I had first accepted Christ when I was sixteen—I had never done something like this. I am more comfortable being in my head, thinking about my faith, rather than acting it out in front of others.

I felt deeply moved, an attraction beyond my control, and drawn to the cross. I started down the aisle very slowly, not knowing what I would do when I got there. I smelled incense burning, probably myrrh since that is our pastor's favorite. I heard the organ playing "Amazing Grace" softly in the background. And I simply kept putting one foot in front of the other. When I reached the end of the aisle, I walked up the two steps to the altar, and I spontaneously knelt and put my head on the cross. It was rough and splintery against my forehead. I closed my eyes, remained silent, my mind empty, for how long I do not know. Then I thought about my brother, from whom I have been alienated for over three decades. I prayed I might see him again in this lifetime, and that I might be willing to apologize to him, should I see him.

When I finally decided to get up, I suddenly worried I would not be able to. I have spinal stenosis and scoliosis, and getting up with no support would be impossible. The spinal stenosis sometimes causes my upper leg muscles to weaken, therefore making it hard to get up. I managed not to show the vulnerability I felt inside: my legs felt weak, my stomach was churning, and I felt embarrassment and shame over being so helpless. I have always had a hard time expressing neediness. As a child, my father always said, "God helps those who help themselves." This certainly conflicted with what I am trying to learn today, that "it is only by God's grace that we can believe in God." But here was a specific way that I *needed* the cross—to get up off the floor. I leaned on the cross and felt it move slightly. *Oh, great,* I thought. *I'm going to be the one to pull the cross down off the altar.* I never looked at the people standing around the altar, because I didn't want to know if they were looking at me.

With the help of the cross, I finally got up. I made my way back to my pew toward the back of the church. It was with hindsight that I realized how God was present in that event. I sometimes think God has a great sense of humor. I have had a long journey trying to accept my limitations.

This was the most moving Good Friday worship I have ever experienced. During my lifetime, a special part of my spiritual life is the mystery that is part of it. I find that when I least expect it I am surprised by the strong sense of the presence of God, a gift of grace from Her.

THE EMPTY STOCKING

Thirteen stockings hung throughout my home before Christmas—belonging to children, grandchildren, step-grandchildren. Twelve of them were filled, and the receivers of the stockings have taken the contents and the stockings on their way. All but one, that is, the one bearing the name "Pat." That one still hangs empty, alone, unclaimed.

I remember Bob, my therapist in the seventies, telling me, "There is no Santa Claus. If you want your stocking full, you'd best get busy." I was enraged. I had always been taught that someone would take care of me and my needs (male, father, husband), and he had, but with strings attached.

I look at the stocking. I feel sad. Why has no one thought to fill my stocking? I guess my role has always been the "filler."

And so I say to myself, *I know that only God can fill my stocking—take away the longing, the yearning, the emptiness, the disconnection. I know this intellectually. But where are you, God?*

And God said, "I gave you the gift you have asked for for many years—contact from your brother. He sent you his first original business card—such a gift. Such a warm feeling."

Thank you, God.

"And two of your three granddaughters spend time with you. Breanna kept saying how "homey" your place was for Christmas. A gift."

Thank you, God.

THE WIND

"The wind blows where it chooses, and you hear the sound of it, but you do not know where it comes from or where it goes … " The Greek word *pneuma,* translated here as "wind," is the same word used for "spirit," and it can also be translated "breath." The Hebrew word for "spirit," *ruah,* has similar meanings (John 3:8, *Lutheran Study Bible* margin notes, p. 1757).

I sat on the couch in the living room in my condo in Lake Geneva, looking out of the sliding glass doors, watching the weeping willow trees swaying in the breeze, and suddenly I was overtaken with an inner rush and a voice within me that said, "This is exactly like God. You can see the *results* of God, but you can't see *God.* And with that, I began to thank God for her constant presence within and around me.

This is the thread that runs through my life, and therefore through my memoir. I can, with hindsight, see examples of the *results* of what God has done in my life, but I have never seen *God,* at least not directly. The closest I came was in the year 2000, when our *Koros* spirituality group had just begun meeting. (The name we chose, *Koros,* means "dancing" in Greek. We found that to be appropriate since we all loved to dance.) We were a group of eight women who wanted to study the variety of spiritual disciplines together. We studied with our associate pastor, Steve Meysing.

I was going up north on a Saturday, and all during the two-hour drive, I kept praying that I would see and experience God that weekend. After I unpacked, I sat down at the breakfast table, looking out the glass door windows, and suddenly I had a vision of Jesus sitting directly across from me at the table. I saw his warm brown eyes, his long brown hair, and his beard. I began talking to him about my life, some of what I hoped for, and some of the sadness I felt. His voice said, "I am with you always." And I knew that this was true. After about an hour of simply being with Jesus, I started to get restless. In my head, I heard myself saying, *I hope you don't mind, but I'd like to watch the news.* And that was the end of my experience. I have never forgotten it. I have always wondered what would have happened if I had been able to tolerate Jesus's presence for more than an hour. It was as if I thought that I either had to sit in a holy way and be in his presence, or go back to my secular way and not be in his presence— but I couldn't do both at once.

In 1972, when I made the decision to let go of all the bruises, black eyes, and emergency room visits, and chose to pour out the last of the cheap bottles of sauterne, God was involved in that process, working through friends who supported me and got me the help that I needed. I believe that God works through people all the time. My pastor, Ken Olsen, my church friend Carole, and my AA friends, Ivan and Janet, all played roles in my becoming healthy and whole. Why? With hindsight, I believe that my being whole has allowed me to help countless others to get healthy and whole.

And when the pastor referred my first private practice psychotherapy client to me, that Halloween night in 1981, God was there. To this day, I believe that I am a conduit for God. Just like a conduit carries electric current through its wires, I carry God's words through me. Before meeting each client I am going to work with, I always say to God, "Please give me the words to say," and then I don't worry at all about what I am going to say.

I believe God puts things in my mind or heart that I need to address. In the last couple of years, my lack of a relationship with my brother has weighed heavily on my mind. I remember the times that Jim, Carol, and I sat with my mother, before they got married, and my mother would talk about my wonderful and perfect wedding. I can remember being embarrassed, cringing, and wishing she would talk about something else. Jim and Carol decided they did not want me in their wedding; today I can certainly understand why. How awful it must have been to sit and listen to all of the stories about my "perfect wedding." Even though my *marriage* was far from perfect!

Actually, there was a long history of my parents comparing my brother to me. I played the role of family hero, whose job it was to be successful and to bring accolades to the family in order to cover up the problems that were developing with my parents' alcoholism. Once again, we were the "lookin' good" family, and I was always the "perfect" one. I continued to play the star role, and I am sure that my brother was probably sick of hearing about it.

A year ago, when I put my head down on that rough wood cross by the altar, at the Good Friday service, I prayed a simple and short prayer: "Dear God, please intervene with my brother and me to heal our relationship. Please make me willing and give me the courage, should the time come, to apologize for my behavior that hurt him and Carol." That was it. I knew God would answer that prayer—I just didn't know how.

When I got the Christmas card from Jim, with the business card enclosed, and then an e-mail saying that it was his first original business card, I absolutely knew that God was working in Her usual way. I figured that if he shared his *first* of anything that it must be special. It would be if I had done that. And so it gave me the courage to compose the letter of apology, which I sent.

I once read that Carl Jung said, "I don't *believe* that God exists, I *know* it!" These are my thoughts also. Although sometimes I can feel God's presence more than other times, if I think about it, I really do know God is there. My hardest task is to simply let God be God, and not to always try to be in control. I must remember that God is my pilot, not my copilot.

I don't know how this last episode of my life will turn out, but I do know it will turn out the way it is supposed to turn out. And once again, God will perform some kind of transformation in me that will allow me either to change myself or my perception, and either way, it will be okay.

BELIEF VERSUS FAITH

Articulated belief versus lived faith, or talk versus walk. What role does the tension between these two play in my soul's journey? I say that everything is up to God, but I live as if, and worry as if, everything is up to me. Why do I do this? To attempt to maintain the illusion that I am in control?

It really wasn't until after I was sixty that I began to think about the implications of being in midlife. I can't believe it took me that long, but I just never thought about age. I was in good health, successful in my business, and I just thought it would always continue on. Perhaps it was after I was diagnosed with lung cancer, had my surgery, and actually experienced some limitations for the first time in my life that I began to think about these things. I still pushed through them, continued working out and walking on the elliptical and the treadmill machines, and was praised by all my doctors. I did not want to see myself as vulnerable or controlled by my health problems.

My spiritual director gives me articles on "the second half of life" issues, and I file them away to read later. Am I in denial? I act as if I think I will live forever.

Jung said that "After forty, all questions are spiritual questions." He also said that we can't live the second half of our lives the same way we did the first half. I know I like solitude better in this half of my life.

I talk about a God of love, but when I run around doing, doing, doing, I am responding to a God of judgment. When I think I never do enough, I never *am* enough, I am relating to the critical father that I lived with all my life. And even relating to God as *mother* doesn't solve the problem because my mother always behaved in such a passive and powerless way that I can't imagine her as God. So I have had to figure out a different way. My sponsor Pat and my spiritual director Jan come closest to the way I would want God to be in my life.

MY SPIRITUAL DIRECTOR

"And where is God in all of that?" she asks in her soft-spoken but persistent voice. We sit in her second-floor sitting room, comfortable and nonthreatening. She is wearing a sweater and skirt and knee socks to keep her warm. A slight accent accompanies her speech. Her blond hair is short and simple, and her blue eyes are deep. Eye contact is something she is comfortable with.

Five years ago, when I first made the decision to enter into spiritual direction, I saw Pastor Jan's business card and a short bio about her hanging on a bulletin board in my church. This is the way God sometimes gets my attention. It jumped right out at me and said to contact our associate pastor for more information. I did that, and she recommended her highly. It took me a few months to work up my courage to call her, but I knew I wanted to explore my faith further. I had too many questions and too few answers.

Jan is an ordained Lutheran pastor in the ELCA. She served as pastor of a local church for many years. She is a trained spiritual director. I really didn't know what to expect, and the first time she asked me the question "And where is God in all of that?" my inclination was to answer "Nowhere!" But somehow I knew that was not the right answer. At that time, we met in her office at the church where she worked. I always sat in the rocking chair with the soft pillows and rocked. She sat across from me. Sometimes she began with a gong and we sat in silence. Other times she read a passage to me. I have discovered that I love to be read to, and of course, she is the only person who ever does this for me.

Acceptance and nonjudgmentalness are her greatest characteristics. I have often shared something shameful from my past, only to have her say, "Don't you think there are lots of people who have done that?" And, of course, part of the problem is that I don't . As I have learned over the years to be aware of the feminine face of God, this woman represents what I think God would be like.

She challenges me to change, often to rely more on God's mercy than on my own strength. Her greatest belief is in the power of love. When I tell her things like about my worrying about whether my father went to heaven because I don't know it he accepted Christ, she convinces me to err on the side of God's forgiveness and inclusiveness.

Jan is creative. She uses art forms and pictures to convey messages. Her use of metaphor is exquisite. One of her most creative ideas for my life was for me to get on Facebook so I could communicate with my granddaughters that I never saw. It worked wonders, and now I have a relationship with two of the three girls.

Relationship is what Jan believes God is all about. We are created to be in relationship. I love that.

In February 2007, I had lung cancer surgery. Our pastor was taking vacation time and was not available to come to the hospital. I was a bit discouraged. Jan asked me if I would like for her to come to the hospital and anoint me before the surgery. "Oh, yes," I said. So she crawled out of bed in the dark and got to the hospital before 7:00 AM for the anointing. I felt guilty because by the time she could do it, they had inserted the epidural and I couldn't remember any of it, but she assured me it would "count."

I realize how important this lady is in my life as I listen to how often I quote something she said or mention her in my writing. She has stretched my ability to live with events that are out of my control, and simply to turn them over to God. We talk about the 12-step philosophy, by which I also live. And she is supportive of that.

She shares with me from her own life, especially since I went to Christina Baldwin's writing workshop. She has also taken a workshop with her. She is supportive of my effort to write my memoir.

She suggests things I might do with my grandchildren to enhance our relationships. And she suggests things I might do to feel closer to God. I have always had a hard time journaling, so she has had some helpful ideas, like cutting out things that are meaningful to me and pasting them in the journal.

When I worry about my doubts, she reassures me that if my faith were not strong, I would not be able to tolerate doubts. By the time she finishes, I begin to feel okay about where I am at in my journey.

I thank God that I have found this woman who is wisdom personified, strong yet kind.

EPILOGUE

HANSEL AND GRETEL

My mother used to tell me that I made her read *Hansel and Gretel* to me every single night until she couldn't stand to hear even the title of the story. I thought how my life this last year has been like that fairy tale. In my writing pieces from my past, I have made some trips back into the dark forest, and that is always scary, for fear I will not find my way out. But like Hansel and Gretel, I have had some real live "bread crumbs," like the women in my writing group from last June, who continue to encourage me and also help me find the way out of the scary dark forest and back into the light. I am getting less and less afraid of the dark and more aware of the sources of light and love that surround me. I know now that even my father loved me, as best he could during his progressing alcoholism, and I can feel that love.

Christina Baldwin summarized my story by saying that the threads found in my story are alcoholism, real attachment, and resilience. I try to keep those words in front of me always, for they too will be like bread crumbs to lead me out of the dark forest and into the light.

As I finish this memoir, written to be presented to my nine grandchildren at my seventieth birthday party, I want them to know that no matter what obstacles they meet in their lives, our family has a long legacy of resilience and perseverance, and I pray they will listen for God's guidance and wisdom, both in others around them and also within themselves. I let go of this book and turn it over to God, knowing it will end up where it is supposed to be.